A Blessed Life

Hoan Tran

NEWMAN SPRINGS PUBLISHING
320 Broad Street
Red Bank, NJ 07701

First originally published by Newman Springs Publishing 2024

ISBN 979-8-89061-094-2 (Paperback)
ISBN 979-8-89061-979-2 (Hardcover)
ISBN 979-8-89061-095-9 (Digital)

Printed in the United States of America

In loving memory of Mom and Dad

To my best friend, Diep
*To Harrison, thank you for your unwavering love
and support over the last thirty years, making
it possible for this dream to come true!*

CHAPTER 1

The End!

My friends and I sat in silence at the corner noodle shop, looking at each other knowingly under a well-lit night. The stars were so bright tonight. What a total irony, for we were in the darkest time of our history. The brutal, dragged-out war had taken a toll on us all, albeit, up to this time, I only had to endure it for a little more than a decade. I looked at my friends as if this would be the last chance we would have together. It was a beautiful night, but the air somehow was much heavier, damper, sadder. These were my childhood friends. We had known each other pretty much all of our lives. We grew up together, playing in the streets of our beloved neighborhood. I felt a sense of sadness, disappointment, and desperation. I thought of my parents and how much they must have gone through to always keep us safe in the face of destruction. I was oblivious to much of this, or at least I did not pay much attention to it before now. All I knew was waking up to a loving home, going to school, and playing with my friends. It was a totally innocent life hidden from all the sadness and destruction. My parents made sure I would be shielded from all of it for as long as possible!

Vietnam was a beautiful country with a blend of the big cities with modern architecture from the West, the humble, simple straw huts in the villages to the stunning coastlines of pristine sandy beaches, but few knew it. I always wondered what it would be like to live in the beautiful remote villages where nature reigned supreme, where the air was much fresher and the trees more abundant.

I remember our family's vacation to Vung Tau Beach, one of the more popular cities and beaches in South Vietnam. In the summer, people would flock to this beach for its scenery, hot sand, and warm water. This was a child's dream. This was the one and only time I visited a beach during my childhood. I was six years old at the time. It was special to me for many reasons, the most important of which was spending time with my entire family. Sadly, this vacation came one year before one of the bloodiest attempted invasions of South Vietnam by the North. More to come!

Every time I recall this vacation in my mind, I come to appreciate my parents even more. They knew how difficult life was with the constant stress of the dragged-out war, so they tried, whenever they could, to take us away for a short time to cleanse our minds, lift our spirits, and enrich our souls. They made it work with eight children and a very tight budget. Dad had a friend who owned a nice cabin on the beach and often encouraged my dad to take our family for a vacation there. Dad, dealing with his duties in military intelligence, tried hard to find a good time to do it. It was very difficult, but Dad managed, on this occasion, to take a few days from his wartime responsibilities to bring all of us to the beach for a few days.

I remember thinking, *This is the life!*

I spent hours upon hours in the water, until my skin turned to "prune." The sun was welcoming, the air was fresh, a huge difference from the tight, busy streets of Saigon. My parents took us to eat at the local street food vendors, and they were out of this world. We ate all the Vietnamese specialties—noodle soup, Vietnamese crepes, and all the best seafood my heart desired. It was three days of pure bliss, and I loved every minute of it.

I was usually the one asking my parents from time to time to take us on a vacation without realizing how difficult it was for them to agree, both because of time and financial constraints. I did not realize this (again, I was a young boy!) until I had one of my many chats with Mom. I enjoyed our beach vacation, but I felt very guilty once I found out how difficult it was for Dad to pull it off. I could not even imagine, with everything going on with the war, Dad managed to arrange this vacation for us. A tinge of guilt but mostly admiration for Dad flowed through me whenever I thought about this vacation.

My friends and I lived in Saigon, where all the conveniences of city life were readily available to us. The hustle and bustle of a city full of street shops, restaurants, fruit stands, and souvenir stands were major attractions, not only to many tourists but also to the local folks. They never seemed to shut down. If you were hungry at two o'clock in the morning, you could find street food vendors serving up your favorite food. It rivaled New York City and was truly a city that never slept. This was where I grew up and the only place I had ever known. This was *home*! The only thing I wish I could have had the chance to do is visit the villages and the beaches, but it was hard in the middle of a devastating war. My parents were always able to take good care of all of us kids. Life was simple but happy! This was *home*!

As we gathered around the square, we knew it could very well be close to the end! We did not have to say anything, but we understood. In the days leading up to the fall of our beloved country, South Vietnam, there was something different. We felt it. The normally bustling streets and bright lights of a city once so vibrant were now almost empty, except for a few street vendors and motorbikes cruising as if this was the last chance before everything fell apart. Little children selling lottery tickets and the beggars along the curbsides remained the only presence of normalcy on the deserted streets. It was all coming to an end soon!

I looked at my friends, wondering what they were thinking. We were kids in our teens, and the reality of whether we would ever see each other again weighed heavily on us. All the good and bad times we went through together made it even more difficult to face the inevitable truth that soon, we might never have a chance to see each other again. I looked away, avoiding the emotions I knew ultimately I had to face. I remembered what my dad told me, "Be strong! Life is not all about you. There are other people counting on you." I turned back to look at my friends, and at least for the next few hours, we held hands in silence, knowing this was the "goodbye" we had tried so hard to avoid for so long. We knew, eventually, we must go our separate ways, but this was not how we had imagined.

I finally cracked a smile. "Enough already! It's all going to be fine. You'll see! We are tough, right?" I always seemed to be the one my friends looked to for some sense of calmness and reassurance.

Diep, my best childhood friend replied, "Yeah, we are! Let us make the best of this. The good thing is no more school!"

We all laughed, but we knew we would rather wake up to another brand-new day and see each other at school like every other day. We were interrupted when an elderly lady walked up to us, her back badly hunched.

"Can you boys spare something for an old lady?" she said in a weak voice as if trying to catch her breath. I took out whatever little money I had and gave it to her.

A tinge of pain hit me for I knew no matter what happened, something would never change. The slumps and the alleys would always thrive in a society where chaos seemed to be the only constant. I felt helpless and useless in the face of the most agonizing collapse, not just of a country but of a people who staked their pride on thousands of years of heritage, of courage, and of compassion. It was all coming to an end, and I felt helpless in the face of it all. We were supposed to be the future, the change, and the hope. It was a momentous collapse of the human spirit, and I was a part of it. It tugged at my heart, and for the first time, I felt totally heartbroken and could do nothing but watch it happen.

A little boy walked up beside us. "Do you want to buy some lottery tickets? They're cheap!" he smiled.

What an irony! Here we were nearing the end, and yet this little boy was still hustling for money on the streets. But I guess innocence is a blessing. At least, he would not be able to feel the pain and the disappointment I was feeling now. No matter what happened in the coming days, he would still be on the streets, if he managed to survive the destruction. My friends all dug deep in their pockets and gave the little boy all they had. What would we do with the little money we had anyway? Soon, everything would be totally useless, just as we were!

CHAPTER 2

Moving South

I came from a modest home, with loving parents and seven other siblings, just your typical, average Vietnamese household. My dad, like most men in Vietnam, was in the military serving a country constantly at war for as long as I could remember. I lived under the destruction of the long war the day I was born until the day I left. Yet because of my parents, I was shielded from the true, harsh reality of it all and maintained as much of my innocence as possible. I learned to live as normal a life as I could, sometimes hiding my feelings from my parents. I knew a lot more about the war and how it affected my life and my family than I let on to my parents. I just did not want them to worry. I felt since I had contributed absolutely nothing to the family (well, I was a child then after all), the last thing I wanted to do was to be even more of a burden on my parents. So I tried to live as carefree as I could, as normal as I could, and did the typical things a boy my age would do. I could not tell whether my parents could see through my charade. If they did, they would be good at hiding it since they did not say a word to me. Now, with all that said, I was not an easy boy to handle, wartime or not. It was not an easy undertaking for my parents, given the curiosity and mischievous nature of my personality—in other words, an absolute "troublemaker."

My parents were migrants of sort themselves, fleeing North Vietnam and settling down in South Vietnam in 1954. They grew up in North Vietnam to above-average families and married young. My dad was a schoolboy when he married my mom, and they had their first child at nineteen in 1949. My mom often told me stories about her and my dad's childhood, growing up in a simple town, doing normal things as young teenagers. Unlike me, they were both model children.

After the war with the French, Vietnam was divided into two separate countries by the Geneva Convention. Citizens were given a choice, or so they said, to either stay where they were or to move South. It was a lottery of the sort, given you only had a chance to do it within a given time limit. After that, everyone stayed where they were! No one imagined that the peace treaty called the Geneva Convention would become the start of the most devastating war Vietnam had ever witnessed, even worse than the previous wars with the Chinese, Japanese, and the French. This time, it was different. This time, it was brothers fighting against brothers for what seemed to be pure stupidity if not insanity of opposite principles and egos. As in any war, the people who ended up suffering the most because of the stupid decisions made by the very few egotistical, maniacal, and insane men were the ordinary citizens. This was one of the saddest chapters in Vietnam history, and I bore witness to it, albeit for a short time. But life went on.

My parents decided to take the offer and moved to South Vietnam, despite not knowing anyone there or how life would be there. Something told them they needed to make that journey. My parents were a couple of strong-willed individuals, who were very determined once they made up their minds. So to South Vietnam they went, a young couple in their early twenties, making the long journey with two sons—Huynh, the oldest in the family at five years old, and Dai, the second oldest at four years old—and Tuyet, the third oldest and my oldest sister, who was then two years old. Mom was pregnant with her fourth child and my second oldest sister. My mom would tell me later that the journey was exhausting and long, taking several days. My parents lived on their savings for several months when they got to South Vietnam. Dad settled our family down, while Mom took care of the day-to-day stuff for three kids with one more on the way. They rented a simple, modest house near the city center. It was affordable, and that was all they could manage. Life was difficult at first; Mom told me. They were careful with spending money on food and necessities until Dad could find a job. My parents ended up having four more children for a total of eight, including yours truly, to round out our family.

Dad finally ended up enlisting in the army and remained there until his last day, when South Vietnam fell on April 30, 1975. That was the day we lost the war, and I lost my dad forever at the age of fourteen. He had fallen, serving his country. He passed too soon at the young age of forty-five! I could not comprehend losing him and was in denial for a long time! He died defending freedom, defending the ability for people to make their own decisions, defending the idea that everyone should live with dignity. Dad was a quiet man but when he spoke, people listened. I know I did! He was an idealistic and principled man. He never paid attention to material things. He valued family, and people in general, above everything else. Dad often told me, "Fighting never solves anything, son! Punches never accomplish the things you value in life! Violence never wins over peace. When people get aggressive, you need to remain calm. You may not be able to control the situation, but you can always control yourself." I did not appreciate his words at the time, but with everything he witnessed throughout the war, he knew the simple principle of using peace to conquer violence, using love to conquer hate and aggression, and using common sense to conquer anger. I miss Dad!

After several years of serving in the army, my parents saved enough money to buy a comfortable house for us kids. It was not anything fancy. It was in a blue-collar neighborhood where everyone knew everyone. Every kid in the neighborhood played with one another. It was home! Mom did an extraordinary job of managing the day-to-day stuff of keeping all of us well-fed and comfortable, going to school without any worries! Life was simple, and I loved every minute of it.

CHAPTER 3
Dad

Dad

Dad moved up the ranks in the military and eventually started working for the war intelligence division. He rarely talked about the war to us kids, just with my mom when they were alone. I guess he did not want any of us to feel insecure, scared, or worried. He was a family man through and through, and his daily routine was so predictable, which was a very good thing. The intelligence department assigned a chauffeur/medical assistant to take care of Dad, but we knew him as Uncle Van. He was a very sweet and caring man, with a family of his own, but he always treated us as his kids. He would come over to our home on birthdays, holidays, sometimes bringing his family over. He was loyal and honest and absolutely adored my dad. I remember Dad would tell him sometimes not to fuss too much over him, but Uncle Van could not help himself. He found joy and happiness in doing stuff for Dad, and we enjoyed having him around and saw him as one of our uncles and always part of the family. Every morning, Uncle Van would come over around six thirty in the morning in the military-issued jeep and picked up my dad, and then they headed to the office.

I did not know what Dad's job really involved. I just knew he was very busy taking care of stuff to keep our family safe and serving our country. It was probably for the best since I would only feel worried and scared for my dad if I really knew what was going on. I must have taken after Dad. I sometimes put on a "normal" front to hide a lot of things I was really feeling at the time. I often thought a lot about what would happen to us all when I was by myself in my room, not just our family but everyone in Vietnam, if things got worse, and it did, eventually. People would ask me later how I even managed growing up in that environment. I guess you got to be there to understand and appreciate what was going on. I would tell them, "I just do! That is all I know. I did not have anything else to compare it to. To me, that was "normal." I guess for people who always enjoyed and maybe took for granted the freedom given them, it was difficult to comprehend. For us and many other families, coming home safely at night was not always a certain event. But as kids, we played, we laughed, we cried, we made trouble, just like kids everywhere else in the world. It was life as we knew it in Vietnam. It was *our life*! And believe it or not, I and my friends never had any intention of leaving Vietnam, no matter what happened!

Sometimes, Uncle Van would take Dad home around noon to have lunch with family and took a short and well-deserved break. It was usually a short lunch anyway, and they would head back to the office to finish the day. Most of the time, Dad would not come home until seven or eight o'clock, and dinner for Dad was not the usual dinnertime for others. So Dad would usually have dinner with my mom since she was the only one who could wait that long without getting edgy about it. Mom and my sisters would do all the cooking since the boys in the family were useless when it came to the culinary arts. Our diet was usually made up of a lot of vegetables and fish.

Meat was rarely included in our meals since it was very expensive, and with eight children in the home, it was almost an impossibility. But us kids did not mind it a bit. Dinner at our home was simple but happy. Whenever Dad had a chance to be home early enough, we would gather as a family around an old wooden dining table and talk about our days. It seemed I always took up the most time since something always happened to me every day. Mom and Dad usually let us kids talk, and they would look at each of us, smiling happily. I imagined that as long as we were present at the dining table talking about our stuff, they knew we were good, and that was all they ever wanted for us. I treasured those times, although not at the time. I was certain Mom and Dad were always anxious of all the possible what-if situations.

Dad always gave me the most attention, maybe because I was the biggest troublemaker, and he knew I would be the most likely child to get into trouble. There was even a room in the house named after me for the purpose of a "private conversation" and "punish-ment" when us kids get into trouble. I seemed to occupy that room 80 percent of the time. My sisters, luckily, got the "private conversa-tions" but did not seem to get the punishment whenever they broke the house rules. I often brought this up to my dad, the unfairness and inequity of it all. "Why am I the only getting punished? They broke the rules too, Dad." He would just look at me and say, "You will understand someday, son!" Well, maybe I would understand some-day, but my butt did not understand at the time, and I was a little resentful of the treatment. But the punishment did not stop me from future misdeeds and mayhem I wrecked seemingly routinely.

I remember one time, in sixth grade, which was considered the start of high school in Vietnam, I got into a big fight with a group of kids from a different class. In Vietnam, boys and girls were not allowed to be in the same class. My high school was divided in half by a huge paved path with a big flagpole in the middle; girls on one side and boys on the other. I was glad since I did not care much for girls at that time. I thought they were always trying to get us in trouble with our teachers by ratting on us. I was elected the class president at the time through a lengthy academic selection process. I was supposed to make a good example for my classmates but did not do a very good job of it. At twelve years old, I was very tiny, even by Vietnamese standard, but that did not stop me from talking trash to kids much bigger than me. But this time, it was not my fault—well, not all of it was my fault.

One day, I and several friends were walking home from school, minding our own business. A group of kids from another class headed us off, blocking the main road we were walking on. They seemed tall and big for their age, to me anyway. My friends told me to forget about it and take the small path to the side. Of course, being who I was, I took issue with it and could not let it go. My friends, while hoping I would let it go, were ready to stand by me no matter what happened.

I stepped up to the front. "Can you move so we can go?"

The tallest of the kids in the other group looked at his friends, "Did you guys hear anything? It sounds like a little birdie is chirping somewhere close!" All of them laughed at what I felt was a lame and overused phrase.

I held firm, and so did my friends. "Are you guys going to move or not?" Silence! They kept staring at us as if wanting to pick a fight.

I spoke up again, "We'll give you one last chance to move, or we will move you." That did it. Before I knew what happened, they charged us without saying a word.

My friends and I threw our books down without hesitation and charged them ourselves. We were walking on an unpaved gravel road. There were rocks everywhere. I grabbed a couple of good-sized rocks and went into hand-to-hand combat with the leader of the group. I remember swinging the rocks in my hands wildly at him. I hit him a couple of times. He staggered but did not fall. He retaliated by whacking me in the back of my head with his own rock. I felt something hot running down the back of my neck. I stopped momentarily, feeling the back of my neck. It was hot and red; blood was running down all over my white shirt. He must have seen the anger in my eyes once I saw and felt my own blood. I stood up straight and stared straight into his eyes. Thank goodness he had the common sense to turn around and told his friends to retreat.

My friends fussed over me after, taking me back to the school nurse to have me patched up. We went on our way home after in total silence, but I felt a sense of pride even though I knew I violated the biggest rule my dad set for us kids, "No fighting under any circumstances! Always try to resolve the issue peacefully. Nothing good can come out of escalating the situation, resulting in fighting and violence." I could hear my dad's words clearly in my head. I knew I was in for some pretty good spanking when I got home. But at that moment, with the adrenaline still flowing through my body, I did not seem to care.

My friends walked with me for a short distance, making sure I was good after the school nurse patched me up. I finally got home, obviously a little late and hurting. Almost everyone in my family was present at the dinner table.

Why did Dad pick today to be home early and have a family dinner? I remember asking myself.

I walked in, doing my best to act as though nothing had happened even though there was a big white cloth bandage wrapped several times around my head from the stitching the nurse gave me. Red spots started to seep through the white cloth bandage. My head was throbbing, but I tried my best to pretend it did not hurt.

I whispered, "Mom, I am going to my room to clean up a little and change. I will be right out."

She gave me the classic "I am disappointed in you, son" look but did not say anything. She just nodded and turned back and got the food on the table. My siblings looked at me intensely, partly concerned, partly worried of what Dad would do to me after dinner! But they knew better than to get involved. They knew when Dad was on the "punishment mission," everyone stayed out of the way.

I finally came out to the dining room and sat in my designated spot. Luckily, my spot was not next to Dad, or it would have been even more awkward. Everyone sat in silence for a short time, but it seemed like forever. Here came the part I dreaded more than the punishment itself, sharing your day with everyone. I used to enjoy this part of dinner but not today. Everyone anticipated, by the bandage I had around my head, that I would take up more time than even the usual long time I took normally to explain what happened. But I shocked everyone by keeping it very short, and I did not even mention what led to the bandage around my head. I kept the conversation as short and sweet as I could as if nothing happened. My siblings just looked at each other and wondered what punishment Dad would hand out to me. There was a momentary silence, and my siblings started, one by one, talking about their day. My mind was elsewhere and did not hear one word everyone was saying. I was in my own world. I was not worried about the punishment since I had more of those than I could remember. I was more worried about how Dad was going to feel. I was preparing for how disappointed he would be in me for directly going against his words, his rules. I told my family, after everyone had finished recounting their days, I was tired and would like to go to my room and rest for a little while.

After what seemed to be an eternity, one of my sisters walked in and asked me, "Dad wants to see you. Are you okay?"

I just nodded. I sat on my wooden bed a little while longer before getting on my feet and dragging myself to the "you know what" room to see my dad. A feeling of dread fell on top of me, weighing me down so heavily that I could barely walk. I did not feel my feet moving beneath me, just the sounds of my sandals grinding on the concrete floor. It sounded much better than the way I felt right now. My dad never got angry or raised his voice to any of us kids, no matter how much trouble we were in. I remembered my dad saying once, "I don't want you to miss what I am trying to tell you with being distracted by the anger and the yelling." So he always talked to us kids in the same soothing, calm voice, regardless of whether we were doing something really good or really bad.

I walked through the door of the dimly lit room. Dad had not come yet. I settled into the chair, my usual landing spot whenever I got into trouble. The butt-shaped crater on the chair seat was my size since I was the child who sat there most often. I looked around the room as if it were my first time there. Something seemed different tonight, the air, the feeling, everything! I sat there, eyes closed, head still throbbing, trying to meditate a little to calm my feelings before Dad came. I dozed off momentarily when Dad walked through the door, waking me. I sat up straight as Dad settled himself in his chair across from me. The distance was not far enough between the two seats for my liking.

He started off, "Your head still hurts? We need to get that bandage changed in the morning. I already asked Mom to help you with that." This was how my dad approached all these situations. He would focus on me first to make sure I was okay. My guilt meter went up a few notches as my dad's words registered.

"I am doing okay, Dad. It hurts a little but not bad. Thank you!" I managed to whisper my response.

He just looked at me, worry in his eyes. "Now tell me what happened. Not that it will change the fact that you purposely violated the rules we agreed on. But I still want to know what prompted you to do what you did," he said firmly.

I began telling him the whole story from the beginning to end. He sat quietly for what seemed to be a lifetime.

"You know, you should have listened to your friends. They did the right thing by telling you to forget it and pick a smaller road to get home instead of getting confrontational the way you did. You escalated the situation, son. That is exactly what those boys want you to do. They want to get you worked up. They want to get you angry. And you know when you are angry, you can't think straight, and that was proven again in this situation," he told me, keeping his same calm voice.

"I couldn't help it, Dad. They should not have done that. They...they—"

Before I could finish, my dad cut in, "That is the problem, son. You react to what others are saying and doing instead of controlling the one thing you can control, and that is *you*. You let yourself be consumed by what others do and say. You let them dictate how you feel and how you react. That never ends well. You do what you know is right even at that moment you were angry or do not think it's fair. Everyone gets angry, son. I am not saying you should dismiss your emotions. But by using violence, they get hurt, you get hurt, and the problem remains. Well, you might feel a temporary high of defending your pride—not your honor, just your pride. 'I'm going to show

14

them. They can't do that to me and get away with it.' Was that how you were feeling at the time, son?"

"Yes, Dad," I whispered, knowing he was absolutely right. But I was twelve. I was not very good at controlling my emotions. He should have already known this, right?

"I am not going to punish you tonight. You are in enough pain as it is. I hope whenever your head is throbbing, you can remember what I am telling you now. Can you do that, son?" he said softly.

"Yes, Dad. Thank you!" I responded, trying hard to hide my happiness at not getting punished.

He stood up, came over, and gave me a pat on the back. "One day you will understand this principle more clearly, son. There will be many more situations that will test your will to control your emotions and do the right thing, even if you think it's the hardest thing you will ever have to do." With that he walked quietly out the door. "Try and get some sleep. I know Mom will bring you some medicine to help with the headache."

I remained in my favorite chair, tears running down my cheeks unknowingly, as I tried to digest my dad's words. I knew them to be true, but I was twelve. It would take me a little longer to comprehend the true meaning of what he was trying to say. It would become the cornerstone principle of how I grew up. That was my dad, through and through.

I remember that Dad, in the early seventies, received many foreign guests and dignitaries, given his job at the war intelligence department. One time, he was hosting an event at our house with a member of the Japanese Foreign Ministry. As I said, we lived in a very modest home, but Dad would have the formal living and dining room decorated up a little for this purpose. I was the trophy son, like it or not. Every time Dad had to host an event like this, I would be right there in between Mom and Dad, obviously not knowing how to behave. During this unforgettable encounter, I remember waiting for the Japanese guest for what seemed to be a century that I could not endure the standing. So just as our Japanese guest walked through the door to the living room, I chose that time to sit down in between Mom and Dad. I remember the horrified expression on my mom's face. Dad was busy greeting our guest. Mom bent down a little, trying to pull me up by my arms. I finally stood up, grudgingly. Dad apologized for my behavior, but our guest let out the biggest laugh.

I later found out he told my dad, "I like your son. He's honest and does what he feels like. Kids will be kids, right? That's rare!" I was relieved I avoided an international disaster. During any event similar to this one, we had a photo op to commemorate the meeting. Now that I thought about it, I never looked good in any of those pictures. What did you expect from a twelve-year-old if you forced him to wear *formal clothes* and act *formal*. At this particular event with our Japanese guest, red wine was served. I was supposed to stick to my wine glass filled with water. But I was always too curious for my own good. I remember sneaking out of the living room and going to the kitchen where Uncle Van, the server for the event, was working and asking him whether I could try a glass of red wine. He looked at me, horrified. But I threatened him that if I was not going to have a glass of red wine, I would create a ruckus so loud he would never hear the end of it. He knew I would do it too! He reluctantly gave me a glass of red wine, "Don't drink all of it. Take a small sip, okay. I can get into trouble if your mom and dad find out, and they will if you're drunk."

"Don't worry, Uncle Van. I can handle it." I had this same line I used all the time. At twelve, I thought I was invincible. I could do anything without getting hurt. I could do anything and get away with it.

Massaging the wine glass in my hand, I had this awesome feeling of being a true grown-up, drinking red wine at twelve years old. "Uncle Van, have some wine with me." I smiled at him with an innocent smile.

"I can't, son. I am on the job. I am not allowed to drink while on the job." He bent down to meet my eyes.

"Nobody will know, Uncle Van. Just a couple of sips. You're a grown-up, and a couple of sips won't make you drunk, right?" I tugged on his shirt as I tried to convince him to break the rule.

"Your dad will know. He knows everything. You can't hide it from him," he said anxiously.

"I won't tell," I said with a big smile on my face. Uncle Van looked at me, softening his will as if considering it. He turned around and picked up a glass of red wine on the counter.

"Here's to our family, Uncle Van. I am so lucky to be a part of this family. Aren't you, Uncle Van?" I said, heart full of joy.

"Yes, son. I am, I am!" he whispered as we clinked our glasses softly and started taking a sip, both of us smiling broadly.

Dad was busy talking to our Japanese guest. Mom stayed pretty much silent through the whole conversation. I admired Mom for her willingness to sit through, not just this one, but other formal state events my dad had to host. Her facial expression remained cheerful, no matter how tired she was. Dad appreciated her much more as he often told her after each gathering. She could have made an appearance and excused herself, but she was there the entire time, supporting my dad.

I was the required element that kept these events light and "informal." No matter how serious these foreign guests and the nature of the meetings were, I always managed to make them laugh, through my silly antics and shenanigans. Dad always made a gesture to tell me to settle down, but I knew he was glad I was able to lighten up the mood a little before the serious talks began. I was not old enough to see the purpose of my presence at these state meetings. I was just being who I am and a twelve-year-old boy. Mom would later tell me she and Dad were glad I behaved the way I did, making the state events more manageable for Dad. That got me teary-eyed, to say the least. I was able to do something useful for Mom and Dad, even though it took some of my usual antics to do it.

After his meeting with the Japanese guest, my dad retired to his small study, settling down to his favorite chair that was there for as long as I could remember. I peeked from the room next door. Dad poured himself a nice, hot cup of tea, trying to get some peace and serenity. He closed his eyes, savoring the aroma of the tea steaming up from the cup. I could see the exhaustion on his face. I imagined all the stuff happening around us with the war had him worried for our safety and the future of Vietnam. He never let on how he felt with us kids, but I guessed it was during private times like this he could fully let his true feelings out, albeit just to himself. This was the only way he could release the stress and worries he felt for all of us. I admired Dad for his strength and endurance. But more importantly, I appreciate his love for us kids and Mom. Our family always managed to find the *brighter* side of things, even in the direst of circumstances. A lot of it was because of my dad.

As I mentioned, Dad paid more attention to me than the other siblings in the family, maybe because I needed it with all the crap I pulled seemingly routinely. But one of the things I treasured most, wishing it would have lasted a little longer, was our morning breakfast outings every Sunday. This was our *thing*. This was a couple of hours Dad and me spent every Sunday, going to the same street vendor for hot Vietnamese noodle soup.

Dad would wake me up around six o'clock every Sunday morning, a little too early for me. But for what we were doing, I did not mind one bit. As a matter of fact, I was so anxious the night before I could hardly fall asleep anyway. I would get ready quickly, putting on my most sophisticated outfit, bow tie and all, for this special occasion.

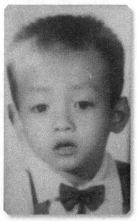

Baby me!

Dad, on these outings, dressed in civilian clothes, and he would put me on his Vespa motorbike and cruise us down the familiar streets to the noodle shop. Traffic was light since it was too early in the morning. I enjoyed sitting behind Dad on his Vespa, arms wrapped tightly around his waist. It took us roughly fifteen minutes to get to the noodle shop from our home, and the ride on Dad's Vespa was my favorite thing.

During the ride, Dad would start telling me about life and how to grow up to be a good person, no matter how tough things got. I did not know if he realized that I was very young and probably could not comprehend most of what he was trying to tell me. Mom would tell me later Dad knew that, but to him, repeating things to me over and over during our weekly noodle soup outings meant I would eventually get it. And he was right! It took a while, but I finally was able to really understand what Dad was trying to tell me. The noodle soup was not bad either.

We would settle into our usual table at the noodle shop. The owner knew us very well since we came every week, at the exact same time, and ordered the exact same thing. The Pho Tau Bay (or Airplane) Noodle Soup had been around for ages, passed down a couple of generations, my dad told me. Dad always recalled the history of places he took me in the hope I could appreciate those places much more. He would be disappointed, at least for several years until I was old enough to appreciate stuff like that.

"You know, son. I know it is not easy for you kids to live under such stressful conditions of war and all. But Mom and I promise you kids will be okay, no matter what," he began our conversation on this day. I looked at him, waiting for him to continue. "You are probably too young to appreciate it now, but when you grow up, you must always be a good person, honor your words, and solve any problems you face with dignity and compassion, even when those situations test your patience and humanity. It is not difficult, son, to stay calm with people and situations you agree with. The real test comes when you are involved in situations and with people you do not agree with. I want to tell you, son, you solve those situations similarly, meaning in a calm and peaceful way. Talking and reasoning to people might be the hardest thing to do, but at the end, it is all worth it," he told me as we waited for our noodle soup.

"Yes, Dad," I spoke softly, stomach growling from the hunger coming from smelling the delicious aroma of the noodle soup. Dad must have known I did not pay much attention to what he was saying.

The sky was bright with sunshine and pale, white clouds. My friends and I gathered in my front yard, lined on both sides with beautiful pots of flowers, flowers my dad personally selected and groomed. Some of the flowers were quite rare and very difficult to care for. Planting flowers and plants was one of my dad's great passions. I guess it gave him a chance to get his mind off the tremendous responsibility of defending our country. He was very particular about his plants and flowers, some of them quite fragile and elegant. He repeatedly told me not to play in the front yard since I could potentially damage his plants and flowers. Somehow, I could not remember his warning on this day.

My friends and I began setting a picnic bench on each end of the yard as soccer's goal posts. We decided to play soccer in my front yard that day. I did not know why, but I felt the urge to do it and invited my friends over. There was a total of eight of us. I would be the goalie for one team. My three teammates promised me they would be extra careful not to damage the flowers. We were ten! What did we know about keeping promises? Nonetheless, that comforted me a little. I smiled at them and said, "It's alright! We'll be fine. The flowers will be fine. Everything will be fine!" I was wrong!

We began running up and down the field, aka my front yard, with the soccer ball between our feet. It was a fierce competition. I looked at my friends and felt very fortunate to have such wonderful people around me, besides my family. I was in a ready stance as the opposing team moved the ball closer to my goal. I looked and pointed toward my teammates to tell them to make sure they protected the home goalpost and not let the others come too close. *Too late!* As I looked straight ahead, three blurry figures moved with great speed toward my direction. I got down to a crouching position, legs spread, arms and hands forward, I was ready! The forward for the opposing team shot the ball with great speed and force. In a quick instant, I reacted. I twisted my body sideways and folded my hands into two fists. With all my strength, I lunged at the ball with both fists, knocking it to the right of the goal. I smiled with satisfaction at the fairly nifty save. I could tell my friends, with their jaws open in awe, were impressed. That gave me even more confidence. I quickly realized that those were not looks of admiration but of shock. It did not last long before I finally realized they were horrified because the ball had accidently destroyed one of my dad's beloved flowerpots. Now it was my turn to wear the expression of shock on my face. Of all the stupid things I had done in my life, this would rank in the top three. I was not thinking about the punishment (well, a little!) as much as I was thinking about how disappointed my dad would be (a lot!). I looked at my friends as none of them was still in the mood to play. They gave me their conventional condolences as they left me standing there by myself to contemplate my fate. I waved at them goodbye, absently, as I turned and walked back into the house. It would be a few hours before my dad got back from work, and a brilliant idea crossed my mind (well, at least it was brilliant at the time I thought of it).

I ran into the kitchen and retrieved a pair of strong and sturdy wooden chopsticks. I gathered some clear tape and wires.

Running back out to the front yard, I thought, *This will be great. Everything will be fine!*

I carefully measured the broken stem of the flower and gently put the chopstick behind it. Holding the flower upright against the chopstick, I began wrapping the thin, light wires around it from the top of the stem to the bottom. I wrapped the clear tape around the entire gadget to make sure it held. I then deliberately pushed the injured flower behind the healthy ones to mask the damage.

Dad would never know, I thought.

I was heading down a slippery slope without brakes and didn't even know it. I smiled at my accomplishment as I stared at the beautiful handiwork I just did on the flower.

He would never know! I thought.

I walked back into the house, with a swagger this time, knowing that everything would be fine, and I could get away with one.

I was in my room, doing my homework for the next day. There was a knock on the door. My heart started pounding, and all of a sudden, I didn't feel as confident as I did earlier in the day. I quietly stood up from my bed and opened the door. Just as I feared, my dad was standing in the doorway. He didn't look upset or angry. That gave me some hope, momentarily.

He asked, "So how was your day? Anything interesting happened today?"

"No, Dad…nothing exciting! Just the same old stuff!" I answered, sensing a light trembling in my voice.

"Really! So everything is going great?" he repeated.

"Yes, Dad! Everything is great!" I tried to compose myself

"Well, good. Glad to hear that," he said gently and turned as if to leave.

I could feel my heart drop to the pit of my stomach, from relief I guess. Or is it something else? Suddenly, he turned back.

"Oh, by the way, for some strange reason, I noticed there was something wrong with the rare flower I planted in our front yard. You wouldn't happen to know anything about that, would you, son?" His voice remained very gentle as he spoke.

"What do you mean, Dad?" I continued down the slope and couldn't stop.

"Son, I know. You wouldn't happen to be responsible for that little incidence, would you?" He sounded disapproving now.

I just looked down to the ground, unable to speak. I kept my eyes on the ground as I finally managed to answer, "Yes, Dad. I did it. I am so sorry, Dad!"

"We'll talk later about your punishment," he said, his voice full of disappointment.

At that moment, I didn't know whether I felt bad thinking about the punishment or even worse at the look on my dad's face, full of disappointment. I flopped back heavily on my bed, face down. I just lay there for the next couple of hours, contemplating and reflecting on what I had done. It made me feel even worse.

There was a gentle knock on the door, dragging me back to reality. I grudgingly stood up and opened the door. My mom stood there with a tray of food. She looked at me lovingly and said, "Well, you still have to eat, don't you?" The smile on her face made the feeling inside me even more painful. I disobeyed my dad, and what was worse, I lied to him about it afterward. I guess when you're ten, you did the first thing that came to mind, especially when you panicked. Everything seems a big deal when you're ten! I took dinner from my mom as she kissed me. I looked at her briefly but turned away to avoid crying. She gently closed the door and left me to reflect some more on what I had done. This was actually worse than any punishment my dad would hand me later. The silence, the reflecting, and the disappointment weighed heavily on me. I set the tray on the floor, next to my bed. I managed to climb back onto my bed and fell into a deep sleep, the kind for the emotionally drained and exhausted!

Dad spoke to me the next day, still not angry, but I could tell he was absolutely disappointed. "Son, I don't think it's necessary for me to remind you of what you have done. But I am curious as to why you did what you did."

"I don't know, Dad. I guess in that moment, I just did it, not thinking," I answered him honestly.

"Did you ever stop to think of the possible consequences? Or at least thought about what I told you?" he asked me in a sincere voice

"Yes, Dad, I did. But somehow, I ignored them and did what I did anyway. I don't even know why," I answered Dad, again very honestly.

If anyone understood how my mind worked, it would be Dad. He knew there was something off at times with how my mind worked, but at the same time, he told me a few times that made me unique and made me who I was.

"I know how your mind works, son. But you have to stop sometimes and think of the consequences. This time, it's only the flowers, but what if something bigger was involved, a person, for example. What would happen then?" he said with urgency in his voice!

"I know, Dad. I am so sorry. I guess I wasn't thinking. I know you always teach me to be mindful because it's not always about me, and I need to think of others. I am ready for my punishment. I just hope you are not too disappointed," I finished up the conversation.

He put his hands on my shoulders. "As long as you know that, son. That's all I want anyway, for you to learn. While it might seem small and insignificant now, it will have bigger consequences later when you deal with bigger problems in your life. Understand, son?" he reminded me one last time.

I just nodded, and though he did not give me a formal physical punishment, his words pained my heart the way I had not felt before. Dad had a way of doing that, and I appreciated every moment of it.

Dad passed away at the tender age of forty-five, when I was fourteen. It was the most devastating time of my life. Everything he taught me came to full view as well as the regrets I felt for not paying them any mind. The ultimate sacrifice for a military man is knowing once you signed up to defend your country and protect your people, your life is no longer your own. He accepted it willingly and proudly.

"Don't ever be afraid to do the things you feel are right! Your life is not about what you have but about how you live it!" Dad would tell me often.

The most devastating part of it all was me not being there, not being able to be with him when he passed. The cruelty of war was on full display, with the final act of ultimate insult.

CHAPTER 4

Mom

Mom

Mom was born on the year of the snake, strong and independent by nature. In the face of adversity and challenges, great or small, her steely demeanor and spirit was what kept our family together, while Dad was busy defending it. Initially, she did not want to come to America; she firmly believed the only place she belonged to until the end was Vietnam, with Dad. But ultimately, she did come to America because of us kids. She rarely showed her true feelings, always wearing a smile to protect the innocence of her children. She never wanted her children to feel threatened or afraid of the adversity and atrocities happening around them. Dad loved her very much, and she loved him just the same. Sometimes they didn't need to talk to know what the other person was thinking or feeling.

Mom and Dad on a date

They married young and had kids early. Mom devoted her life to raising us kids and did a damn great job of it, from the long journey southbound in 1954 with my oldest brother, Huynh, five; my second oldest brother, Dai, four; and my oldest sister, Tuyet, two, and pregnant with my second oldest sister, Thu, to settling and building a new life with Dad and their young family in South Vietnam.

Mom was very much a disciplinarian but had a very soft side to her when Dad was handing out punishments to the children, especially me. I took it for granted, growing up in a somewhat normal and loving, except for the *war* thing. Dad would leave the handling of the family's financial stuff to Mom, and she was exceptional at managing it. While Dad held a very prestigious position in the intelligence unit of the military, we lived a very humble life, and he never abused his position for financial gain. This was the principle he shared with me on our weekly Sunday trips to the famous noodle shops (Pho Tau Bay): "always live with *honor* and die with *purpose* and *integrity* because when everything else is gone, honor, purpose, and integrity are the only things you have left. They define who you are, not social status, not material things, not financial wealth." It didn't matter to me at the time, being so young, but it would matter a lot later on my journey through the challenges of life, and I felt a sense of deep gratitude to Dad. I was happy to finally understand what he was trying to tell me and why he decided to share them with me so early in my life.

I often asked Mom what life was like growing up before she moved south in 1954, since I was a South Vietnam baby. She came from an above average family (for Vietnam standards), going to school and helping the family convenience store. My dad, she told me one time, was a very quiet but very charming man. Like most Vietnamese families in that era, many romantic encounters and marriages were prearranged, whether through families who have known one another for a long time or families who used marriage to repay a debt, marrying off their daughters. In that way, my parents were the exception to the rule! They met by chance and fell in love by choice! They grew up in Hung Yen, a city sixty kilometers (thirty-seven miles) south of the capital of North Vietnam, Ha Noi.

Mom told me it was a much different time then, so peaceful. She told me how beautiful the city was with the beautiful trees, the gravel roads, the winding countryside, and the lakes, all cozying up to the bright blue sky, much different from the hustle and bustle of Saigon, the capital of South Vietnam. I could literally see the city in front of me even though I had never been there and was only six years old. Mom was a very good storyteller. She could paint the images with her words to give her listeners a vivid picture of where she was taking them. She had the perspective of the differences between the two cities. While I did not have the same perspective, she gave me a strong appreciation of the differences. It was as though I was there, listening to her words and looking through her eyes. This was one of my favorite times, listening to Mom telling me her life story growing up. It was amazing and forged a strong bond between us.

I knew she was a very strong, independent woman but, at the same time, attentive to the needs of her husband and family. I admired her for the way she handled life in general. She was the absolute glue that held our family together, especially at the time when my dad was totally occupied with his work protecting our country.

She always had a very bright, beautiful smile on her face. One time, I remember asking her, "Mom, why don't you smile like that in your pictures? In all the pictures, you look so serious!" She would smile her familiar smile and rub my hair, not giving me an answer. But looking into her eyes, I could tell she was a very caring, romantic, wise, strong woman. She was not one for talking a lot in public but always had time to sit down and teach her children through her stories. She would always end her stories to me with her famous "So, son, what's the moral of this story?" as I was scrambling just to keep up with the details of the stories. Even the stories about her life had teaching moments in them.

As with other typical Vietnamese families around that time, Mom stayed home, taking great care of the children, doing all the cooking and shopping, while Dad was tied up at the military quarters, handling the details of how to keep the country safe along with other brave officers! I got to spend most of my childhood around Mom instead of Dad, although he made time for me whenever he could. I grew much closer to Mom, and while she would not say it, I knew I was more than a handful.

Growing up is a privilege in Vietnam, and I took it very seriously. I remember when I turned ten, Mom and Dad made a very big deal about it, so big that we even had ice cream to celebrate the special occasion. Mom, showing her trust in me, began handing off the grocery shopping to me. I have not forgotten it and was plenty resentful about it. I remember telling my mom, "If this is what it means to grow up, then I'd rather not grow up for a long time!"

The school system in Vietnam was much different from America. We had school six days a week, with only Sundays off. Students from ninth to twelfth grade would have school from nine in the morning to noon, and students from eighth grade or lower would have school from one to five in the afternoon. With all my older sisters going to school in the morning, Mom explained, I ended up winning the jackpot as the *grocery shopper* for the family.

Mom would give me a list of things to get every morning and enough money to get them. In Vietnam, we bought grocery fresh each day; no refrigeration required. I rode my bicycle, which was a small converted motorbike with the engine removed and the basket in front, to the neighborhood open-air market to get the needed grocery every day. Mom told me, "Make sure you bargain for everything you buy. They really bump up the price, and with the fact that you are young, they will take advantage of you every chance they get."

I thought to myself, *They haven't met me yet. There's no chance they can take advantage of me!*

Even though Mom did not teach me to pick out the fresh stuff at the market, I managed to do it well the first time as Mom said, "Good job, son. Did you bargain for these?"

I looked at her, my pride hurt, "Yes, Mom. It was not a problem."

I would precalculate everything Mom gave me to buy on the list prior to heading out to the market. I calculated in my head too: *If I can bargain all this stuff good enough, I will have some money leftover to buy some snacks!* I will not ever forget the first bargain I made in my life. The market had many vendors selling the same stuff, so shoppers had choices of where to get the best stuff at the lowest price. I was on a bargain-hunt mission. My first item on the list was catfish. Catfish was one of the cheapest things you could buy and delicious too. I stopped at the first vendor, and she waved her arm, signaling me to come in closer.

"What do you want today, son?" she said loudly, and the entire market would hear her voice, echoing through the different tents at the market.

"I need two kilograms (roughly four pounds) of fresh catfish, ma'am!" I told her, hanging on to my bike firmly as people were pushing their way through the tight space between vendors.

"You come to the right place, son. I got the freshest of catfish you can find at this market and at a reasonable price," she said with a big smile on her face. She was a short lady, maybe around 1.37 meters (or roughly four and a half feet tall), wearing the typical pajama-like outfit with one leg pant rolled up to her knee and bare feet. She picked up a couple of catfish and got very close to my face to show me. I was jolted and backed up a little on reflex. The smell of the fish stank, and I had to put my arm across my nose to shield it. She could tell I was an amateur shopper. She was wrong!

"I will take 3,000 dong (roughly $3 USD) for these two here, roughly two kilograms, fresh and cheap. You won't find catfish this fresh and this cheap anywhere else in this market, son," she said loudly, again with a big smile.

"Let me think about it, ma'am," I told her and started pulling my bike out of the aisle. I was maybe a few steps off when I heard her calling me.

"Come back, son. Don't be so hasty. Since you are a nice boy, I can let you have them for 2,800 dong, okay?" She softened her voice a little.

"Uhm…that's still too high. Mom didn't give me that much money, and I have to buy a lot of stuff," I told her in my "I love to, but I can't" voice and expression. I stood there silently to try and make her feel a little uncomfortable.

"I can understand that, son. Maybe 2,700 dong. That's as low as I can go." She held the two catfish in her hands, looking at me intensely.

I looked at my shopping list as if trying to figure it out, but I already got a number in mind. I think the silence really did make her uncomfortable.

I finally looked up from the piece of paper, "I can only afford 2,500 for both of them, ma'am, and no more!"

She became a little agitated but managed to answer me softly, "The lowest I can do is 2,600 dong, son." This earned her another "I would, but I can't" look as I turned and started walking away with my bike. This time, she let me walk a few steps more than my previous walk away before calling after me.

"Alright! You got it. It's 2,500 dong for both. You know what, son. You drive a hard bargain. Who taught you how to do that?" she said, clearly annoyed, or was it admiration.

I finally gave her a wide, bright, beautiful smile and said, "Thank you, ma'am. I appreciate your kindness." She could not help but smile back. I scratched off my first item on the list. On to the vegetables.

There was nothing on the list I bought that I did not bargain hard for. When I scratched off the last item on Mom's list, I smiled satisfactorily for I knew there was still some money left in my pocket for a well-deserved snack.

I told myself, *You worked hard, very well deserved!*

With that thought, I stopped at the vendor with all my favorite sweet desserts. I ordered the black jelly with basil seeds in sweet syrup and coconut cream, my all-time favorite! I sat down on the very small, low stool, the sun beating down the back of my neck, waiting for my dessert to come. It did not seem as hot today as it was on other days. The dessert finally came, the ice in it melting instantaneously as the server sat it down on the low steel table. It did not take me long to devour the whole cup—a matter of seconds. It hit the spot perfectly. Wiping my mouth with my arm, something Mom always said to never do, I stood up, pulling my bike out of the aisle, and started to head home, singing along the way. Life as I knew it was simple, and I loved every minute of it.

Life was much harder for Mom and Dad when they headed to South Vietnam, back in 1954. They were financially comfortable before making the move. But they did not complain once or talk about the what-ifs. They just worked hard to do whatever they could to take care of us.

Mom was a symbol of strength. Back then, the Vietnamese culture, like many others, did not value the contributions women made to their families, society, and the world. Looking back at all the years growing up, without Mom's strength and resilience holding our family together so Dad could focus on his own work, I could not imagine where we would have ended up. Dad, unlike many men in the Vietnamese society at that time, always appreciated all the hard work and effort Mom put in every single day to take care of us kids and make things work, and he told Mom often. He brought Mom flowers, chocolate, even when it was not a special occasion, just to say thank you. This was the environment I grew up in, and I unknowingly soaked up the principles of how to be a good person.

My oldest sister once told me I had a near-death experience and how Mom, with her uncanny maternal instinct, got me through one of the most critical times of my young life. My sister Tuyet told me it was a miracle and that I was given a second chance at life. It happened when I was five years old. I was playing in the backyard when I collapsed.

Mom called a taxi and rushed me to Louis Pasteur hospital (a French-run hospital) because it was the closest to our home and happened to be one of the best and most expensive. Not knowing all of this, Mom's priority was getting me treated immediately. She was not the type to panic. She got me admitted to the hospital, and all she could do was to wait, my sister by her side. Mom was very worried but trying her best not to show it. Mom was not much of a "wear your emotions on your sleeves" person. After a while, the doctor and nurses came out and told Mom to get settled in because they had to admit me for a couple of days for observation.

Detecting a sense of worry, they told Mom, "Don't worry, ma'am. It's only for precautionary purposes. He's doing well and resting comfortably. We think there is something going on with his gut, and it's causing some pain. We took some X-rays and should know soon. We gave him some pain medication in the meantime to give him some relief."

"Thank you, doctor! Can I see him for a little bit?" Mom's voice steady but anxious.

"Give us a few minutes to get him checked in. We will come and get you once he's ready. Again, don't worry. He's going to be fine," the doctor assured Mom.

Mom went back to the waiting room and sat down next to my sister, telling her everything. She let out a much-needed sigh of relief.

"We need to go home after we see Hoan. I have to pack a few things and come in to stay with him. He will be here for a couple of days for observation," Mom whispered softly to my sister. My sister just nodded and held Mom's hands tightly, cracking a little smile of relief herself. They sat there for what seemed to be an eternity before a nurse came out.

"You can go in and see him now. But please don't stay too long. He needs his rest. You can come back later if you want when the medication wears off a little," she told Mom and my sister with a soft smile.

"Thank you. We will." Mom and my sister walked alongside the nurse to the recovery room where I was admitted, looking straight ahead.

The room was small but enough for Mom and my sister to sit down next to me on either side. Mom, putting her hand on mine, squeezed it softly. "You will be fine. Everything will be fine. You will go home with us soon."

I was in a deep sleep from the medications they gave me, not knowing anything going on around me. My sister was there not only to make sure I was fine but, more importantly, to support Mom. More on my sister later, but she was also a strong person, not letting her emotions show. Besides Mom, she was the one handling all the household chores, keeping the home clean, washing clothes, and was Mom's assistant cook and all-around phenomenal sister. Mom and my sister Tuyet sat in silence, looking at me resting. At least for now, there was no immediate threat. Tuyet told me later that they sat for a couple of hours before the nurse came back and told us to leave since visiting hours were over. She told Mom they would transfer me to another room on a different floor later that evening, and Mom could come and stay with me overnight. Mom nodded in agreement, thrilled that she would be able to spend time with her son. It was dark when Mom and my sister walked out of the hospital, waving down a taxi, and headed home. Things would be worse the next day for me, but for now, they felt a sense of relief and comfort that everything worked out. The sky was darker than usual, with soft rain starting to fall and the mood much lighter.

"Everything will be fine," they whispered to each other!

"How is he? What happened?" Mom caught an earful as all my siblings were talking over each other, wanting to get the latest updates.

"Hoan is fine. He's resting comfortably. They gave him some medications, so he was a little sleepy. Probably good for him though since they were trying to help him with the pain. They said they think it has to do with his gut, but they won't know for sure until they have the X-rays back." Mom told everyone the details as she settled into her chair, next to Dad.

"When can we see him, Mom?" Dai, my second oldest brother spoke.

"Well, they only allow one person to come in. They said they're moving him to a semiprivate room, and I can stay with him overnight. I will let you kids know when I get more. Don't worry. He's fine!" Mom said reassuringly, but everyone still had a worried look on their faces.

"I am tired. Let's eat. Looks like you are all hungry. I will pack some clothes and head back there early tomorrow morning. Take care of Dad while I am gone. It shouldn't be but a couple of days, the doctor said." Mom stood and walked to the kitchen, my oldest sister, Tuyet, followed her.

Everyone ate in silence. There was no "share your day" stories from everyone. They were preoccupied with how I was doing.

Dad held Mom's hand in a soft squeeze. "Don't worry, Mother. Everything will be fine. Knowing him, he's too much of a troublemaker to stay there long." He smiled softly, helping lighten the mood a little.

All my siblings smiled along with him. Mom let out a soft, obligatory smile, but deep down, she was still worried. There was plenty of food left this night since no one had the usual appetite of the previous nights.

Dai finally spoke up, "I will take you to the hospital tomorrow, Mom. Why don't you pack and get some sleep. You had a very long and exhausting day." Dad came over to help Mom out of her chair and walked her to their bedroom.

"Come on, Mother! Let's get you to bed so you can have energy for tomorrow. It will be a long day for you." He leaned over and gave her a gentle kiss as they disappeared behind the bedroom door.

My siblings sat around the dining table for a while, talking about their day. They worried about Mom. Dai spoke up, "I will take Mom to the hospital tomorrow and stay in the area just in case. I will let Mom know tomorrow so if she needs anything, I can fetch it for her."

"That would be great. Let's do all we can to help Mom through this," Huynh, my oldest brother chimed in. He was also a member of the military, and his days started early and ended late, just like Dad's. "Dai, I will swing by when I can and check in with you when I can."

"I will let everyone know if there is any change from the hospital," Dai spoke softly

"Now, let's all go to bed and get ready for tomorrow." Huynh motioned everyone to get up and go to their respective bedrooms. My four sisters shared two rooms, and Huynh, the oldest, got his own room. I shared a room with Dai, my second oldest brother, even though we were eleven years apart.

All my sisters stood and cleared the table, taking all the dishes to the blue dishwashing tub in the backyard. Thu, my second oldest sister, washed the dishes, and Thuy, my third oldest sister, rinsed and dried the dishes in the yellow rinsing tub. Tuyet packed the leftovers in containers in the kitchen. They would have to eat them by tomorrow before they went bad, without refrigeration. Life was very simple, and I loved every minute of it.

The neighborhood rooster crows loudly and clearly every morning, right around six o'clock. But today, Mom was already up since four o'clock, beating the rooster at his own game, rendering him quite useless. My sister Tuyet was already up as well, putting a hot pot of tea on the stove so my Mom would have some caffeine in her for the long day ahead. The aroma of the jasmine tea was tantalizing, sweet and flowery. Mom sat in her chair in the softly lit dining room. Tuyet brought the two teacups and saucers to the table and a small dish of sugar cubes. She sat one by Mom and the other for herself, on the opposite side. The iron teapot steamed heavily, letting out a small rhythmic hiss. The tea was ready. Tuyet poured Mom the first cup, then sat down. She took a little longer to pour hers, after she put two small sugar cubes in Mom's cup. She stirred for her.

"Drink the tea, Mom. It will make you feel better. Everything will be fine. He will be home soon," she told my mom, her voice very reassuring.

"I know. But I hope the doctors can tell us what's happening to Hoan. Hopefully, the X-rays are clear, and he gets to go home sooner rather than later," Mom whispered softly.

For a while, they sat in the dining room in silence, waiting for Dai to wake up and take Mom to the hospital to check in on me. It is at times like this that one can understand the strong bond between mothers and their children. Without speaking a word, Mom and my sister understood one another's thoughts and feelings. That bond would never be replicated anywhere else but between mothers and children.

Dai broke the silence as he walked into the dining area. "Ready to go, Mom?" He gave Mom's shoulders a soft squeeze. Mom nodded as she stood up.

"Take care of your dad while I am gone, Tuyet," Mom whispered her final instructions of the day as Dai took her by the arms out to the backyard where his motorbike was parked. Fastening Mom's bag to the front steering and giving her a safety helmet, they were off to the hospital, the sky still dark.

They arrived at the hospital after roughly thirty minutes. The parking lot was fairly empty, with a couple of street food vendors setting up their food stands. The smell of sweet rice filled the parking lot and Dai felt hungry.

He told Mom, "You want some sweet rice, Mom?"

"I am not hungry, but you can get some for yourself. You need to eat since you're going to hang around for a while." Mom looked at him lovingly.

"Okay, Mom. We should be able to get in there in about another thirty minutes. I will go in with you and make sure you get settled into his room." Dai smiled broadly at Mom while waiting for the sweet rice he just ordered.

"I will be fine. You don't have to hang out here all day. You can go home and come back in a few hours. Let the nurse know when you are in the lobby, and I can come out and meet you to give an update. You're wasting time sitting out here in the parking lot anyway. Not much you can do," Mom told him.

"Okay, Mom. I will see how things go. I am fairly free today, so it's not a big deal," he told Mom.

"Okay, but go home from time to time to check in to see if there is anything your sisters need at home." Mom was being Mom.

"Yes, Mom. I will." With that, Dai dove into his steaming sweet rice, savoring the flavor and aroma. They stood in silence, looking at the dark sky above. Today will be a long day.

Mom later told me things turned for the better during my stay. She was finally allowed to come up to my room and check on me. I was doing better but still in some pain. Mom propped up the pillows as she fussed over me. Well, I was five, okay! She pulled up the blanket, afraid I was cold. She pulled stuff out of her bags, including some of my favorite toys. For only a couple of days' stay, she sure brought a lot of stuff. I did not mind it, though. Hospitals in Vietnam are much different from those in America. The rules were not very strict when it came to visitors staying overnight and bringing stuff into the patients' rooms. Mom settled in the chair next to the top of my bed, pulling it closer so she could hold my hand. I smiled broadly, though it really hurt to do so. I was still a little groggy from all the medications the medical staff gave me last night.

After a little while, a nurse came in to take my vitals, changing out the bag of medicine hanging and dripping into my left arm. I was tiny at five; Mom told me, and from the picture I saw later, she was very accurate. Mom said I did not like the food they served in the hospital. She already got some of my favorites packed in her bag. I could smell them when she came in. My mouth, though, was dry and tasted odd.

"He's improving. Do you need anything while you are here with him, ma'am?" the nurse asked my mom gently.

"No. I am fine. Thanks for asking. I'm just glad he's doing better," Mom said softly, smiling at the nurse.

I fell back into sleep for the next couple of hours, the effect of the medication taking a hold of me. When I woke up, I said, "Mom, I am hungry!"

"Okay, son. Let me see what we have here for you to eat." She smiled a radiant smile, the one she showed in a lot of pictures I had seen. This was quite rare for her, but she smiled today.

"Thank you, Mom!" I managed to answer her weakly.

"Don't talk. You gotta rest so you can get better, okay?" Mom rubbed my tiny arm as she whispered to me. I just nodded.

She dug in her bag, pulling out the stuff for noodle soup, my favorite! The aroma filled the room and got me hungrier. She put them on the table next to my bed and started to put it together. She carefully cut the noodle strands into short, manageable pieces before pouring the soup into the bowl. I licked my lips in great anticipation. She pulled the pillow up to the headboard and straightened me up against it, sitting up. She put the noodle soup on the little tabletop attached to my bed and pulled it up to my chest.

"Eat slowly. Make sure you chew everything carefully," Mom said, again smiling. I did not pay any attention at that time. The noodle soup totally took me over. If I was not so weak still, I could finish it in a matter of minutes. But still, I dug in enthusiastically, consuming all the noodle soup Mom made. Satisfied at last, I let out a big sigh of joy.

"Thanks, Mom. That hits the spot." I smiled, revealing a couple of my missing teeth.

"Stay sitting up for a little while longer so the noodle is digested, then you can lie down." Mom cleared the bowl from the table, sliding the bed tabletop down to the end of the bed.

I rubbed my stomach, stuffed, content, and satisfied. Mom stood and headed for the sink on the far side of the room. She started washing the dirty bowl and utensils in the big sink, drying it with the paper towels. She turned and walked back to my bed. Apparently, I was so satisfied or maybe it was the effect of the medications again; I fell asleep soundly. She pulled the blanket over me again, afraid I would be cold. She told me later she never saw me sleep that good before. She was glad, for the worse thing Mom feared was I would be awake and feel the pain. She sat back in her chair, pulling a book out of her bag, and started reading. She, too, would fall asleep shortly after, definitely from exhaustion from fussing over me the last few days. A few hours passed before she woke, checking in on me, of course. She went back to her book for the next hour or so until I finally woke up myself.

She looked at me. "How do you feel?" she said with a gentle smile.

"I feel good," I said.

"Hey, Mom, can you take me outside for a little fresh air?" I asked, anticipating.

"Well, I don't know. I guess we can go outside for a little bit. But let me check with the nurses first, ok?" Mom stood and went out of the room to catch up with the nurses on duty.

Mom returned after a few minutes as I anxiously waited for her answer. "We can go outside for fifteen minutes," Mom finally said to my delight. "But we have to take it easy. No running or any of that." She was stern.

"Yes, Mom," I answered, already putting on my sandals.

Mom put a woven hat on my head, putting a small scarf around my neck to make sure I was warm enough. I guess I was not very good at being kept inside for any amount of time. Mom took me by my hand, and we started walking out of my hospital room. She walked deliberately slow so I could not run ahead of her. I did not mind since the whole idea was for me to breathe some fresh air. The hospital room dragged me down emotionally and I did not want to be the "sick" kid. Even today, the thought of hospitals still gave me the creeps. I took very strong and deep breaths, my Mom recalled, taking in as much as I could as though I had been deprived of it for a long time. I felt resurrected as I walked with a spring in my steps. Mom was happy to see me feeling better. We did not walk far from the hospital, and Mom stopped a couple times on purpose to make sure I did not overexert myself.

After about five minutes, Mom turned. "Let's walk back. The nurses told us we only have fifteen minutes," she reminded me.

"Okay, Mom. But can we sit outside for a little while? I don't really want to go back in that room," I pleaded with Mom.

"We'll see. I can check with the nurses when we get back," she said gently.

We walked back in silence, but Mom felt a great sense of relief. Before long, we were back at the hospital front doors. Mom carefully sat me down on the steps and sat down beside me, still holding my hand. I leaned my head on Mom's arm, closing my eyes, enjoying the nice, soft breeze. Suddenly, my head slumped down on Mom's arm, and she immediate picked me up. Blood drained from my face. She rushed back into the hospital, yelling out for the nurses, panicked. This was one of the very few times Mom was ever panicked.

The nurses came running down the hall, yelling out orders. "Clear the way," one of them said as she sped down the short hallway.

She finally got to Mom, "Ma'am, I will take him now. Please wait in the waiting room, and I will come down to get you when we find out more," the nurse said as she turned and ran up the stairs, taking me to the emergency unit upstairs.

Mom ran out of the hospital to the parking lot, looking desperately for Dai, my brother. He was not there! Mom squeezed her hands tightly together, scanning the parking lot one more time. She was anxious and scared. She stood there, frozen for a little while, until she spotted Dai, turning his Honda motorbike into the parking lot. He realized something was wrong when he got up next to Mom.

"What's wrong, Mom?" he asked, anxiously

"Hoan collapsed again. I took him for a short walk, with the okay from the nurses. We were sitting on the hospital front steps, when he suddenly collapsed. I took him back in, and the nurses have him now up in the emergency room," she said, visibly upset.

"Everything will be fine, Mom. You'll see." Dai tried to calm Mom down.

"It's all my fault. I should have known better. I shouldn't have taken him outside," Mom said, regret in her voice

"Mom, don't blame yourself. The nurses said it's okay to take him for a short walk. You know Hoan. He will nag you until you give him what he wants," Dai reassured Mom as he told her to wait while he parked his motorbike. In a couple of minutes, he walked back to Mom. "Let's go in. We can wait in the waiting room together. You'll see, Mom. Everything will be fine." With that, he took Mom's hand and led her back to the hospital's waiting room.

They sat in silence for what Mom said was an eternity, wondering if everything would be fine as Dai said. Mom kept looking at the clock on the wall across from where they sat, worried, upset, and hoping everything would be fine. The clock continued to click, minute by minute; mom fixated on it. Time seemed to slow down drastically. They waited and waited. After a couple of hours, one of the nurses came and met them in the waiting room.

"He's stable. We think exposing him to the wind in his condition caused chills, and he couldn't handle it and passed out. The doctor will be here shortly to give you all the details of what we have observed the last couple of days. And don't worry. He's doing great." Realizing the worried look on her face, the nurse tried to ease Mom's concerns.

"Thank you!" Mom whispered weakly, exhausted.

Mom and Dai settled back into their chairs, waiting for the doctor to come and let them in on the details. A few minutes passed, and a man in his midfifties walked in and greeted them.

"Hoan is doing fine. He's stable. The lab tests revealed he's losing blood, and we took several X-rays, checking for internal bleeding. Strangely enough, we could not find anything that would suggest he's suffering from internal bleeding. We paid particular attention to the gut area since he experiences some pain there but still couldn't find anything. We would love to keep him here for another day or two to see if we can find anything and just to be sure he does not have any issues. We had begun the blood transfusion to get his blood count back up where it needs to be." He spoke slowly and clearly, making sure Mom and Dai could understand.

"Do you have any question, Mrs. Vu?" the doctor asked. My mom's maiden name was Vu. In Vietnam, unlike in America, when women marry, they do not take their husbands' last name. Another bit of irony: Vietnam was a male-dominant culture where women's contributions were not valued much, yet they could keep their names as a sign of independence, not belonging to their husbands. Anyway, I digressed!

"So he will be fine, doctor? Is there anything else wrong?" Mom asked, still very much worried.

"No, Mrs. Vu. He's pretty healthy. We will make sure to check out everything. He should go home in a day or two. We think he will recover fully." The doctor gently patted my mom's shoulder to reassure her.

"Thank you, doctor, for everything," Mom said, genuinely grateful. He turned and walked out of the waiting room. Dai gave Mom a big hug, relieved and happy.

"Let's go home, Mom. There's nothing more we can do here. Hoan will be fine. He always is!" Dai took Mom's arm, and they slowly walked out of the hospital to the parking lot.

"Are you hungry, Mom?" Dai checked in on Mom.

"No, I am good, son. Let's go home!" Mom said, managing an awkward smile.

All my older siblings were anxious when Mom and Dai got home. "How is he? What did the doctor say? When is he coming home? Did they say…" They all clambered to find out the details.

"Will you guys stop! Give Mom a break. Can't you see she's exhausted?" Dai said sternly.

"Sorry!" they said collectively.

Mom sat down at the dining table, and the kids gathered around her. They sat in silence, but all had a clear understanding of each other's thoughts.

Tuyet, my oldest sister, stood up. "I'll make some tea for all of us," she said and then walked into the kitchen. We were a very reserved family. We did not typically display or express our emotions. But we knew we cared for and loved one another unconditionally, especially Mom.

"Get some rest, Mom. Dai will take you to the hospital tomorrow to check in. Hoan will get to come home soon," Tuyet said.

Mom nodded and sipped her hot green tea, the Three Crabs brand, a local Vietnamese favorite. They came packaged in a square bag with the picture of three crabs prominently displayed on the wrapping paper. These are loose-leaf tea. We had many ceramic and iron teapots lying around the house. Mom and Dad were avid tea drinkers, and they were very particular about their teas. Tuyet was the only one in the family who was allowed to make tea for Mom and Dad. She knew how much tea to put in the pot, how much water to mix it in, how long to simmer it on the stove, and how strong the flames should be. We did not have gas stoves as in America. We had small and big clay charcoal stoves, and all cooking was almost always done outdoors.

Cooking had always been a *family event* in most Vietnamese households. It gave the family the chance to gather around the clay stove, the warm flames, the aroma of the foods, talking and sharing stories. When I was old enough to remember, I would always try to be a part of the *cooking* experience as I could with my family.

When I was nine years old, during the Vietnamese New Year in 1970, year of the dog, Mom allowed us to stay up all night with her, cooking the traditional *rice cake*, preparing for the festive occasion. Vietnamese New Year was the biggest celebration in Vietnam. Us kids got two weeks off from school and did nothing but eat and play. As kids, we were given *red envelopes* with money as part of the tradition of bringing luck to our new year.

I sat and watched Mom prepare the rice cakes. She picked the huge banana leaves from our trees in the backyard. I could not count them all, but there were a lot since it took at least two or three full-size banana leaves to make one rice cake.

It was a very complex, labor-intensive process, but the Vietnamese ladies seemed to have it all under control. It took amazing skills and patience, and Mom had both. She started each rice cake delicately with *sweet rice* (the sticky version of regular rice) spread inside a banana leaf. The amount of rice needed to be just right so it wouldn't be impossible to cook. After the sweet rice was placed neatly in the middle of the banana leaf, Mom spread a layer of cooked, finely chopped green beans. Once the rice cakes were done, the green beans became a paste and blended tightly with the sweet rice. Next, Mom put a couple of pieces of bacon on top of the green beans. This gave the rice cake a rich, tasty flavor. Mom carefully wrapped and shaped the rice cakes into squares. The secret, Mom said, is to pack the rice cakes really tight so that when you unwrap them, they stay in the square shapes you wrapped them in. Mom's rice cakes came out almost always perfect, both in flavor and shape.

It usually took anywhere between twelve and sixteen hours to cook the rice cakes in a huge pot over a very intense flame, usually using wood and tree branches. When she was finally done putting the rice cakes in the pot and lighting up the flames, Mom stayed seated, making sure she fanned the flames often to keep the fires going and the rice cake constantly heated and cooked.

While the rice cakes were being cooked, Mom would have me sit close to her, and she would start telling me stories of long ago. This was my favorite part of staying up with Mom, making rice cakes.

Mom finally finished her tea and headed back to her room.

Dai spoke up, "Get some rest, Mom. We will go to the hospital early tomorrow." His smile gentle and warm. Mom just nodded.

Dad was working late tonight, pulling an all-nighter at the intelligence war room. Mom usually worried a lot for Dad, afraid he worked too hard, affecting his health. But tonight, she was occupied with my condition. She took it all in stride, knowing my Mom.

Again Mom beat the rooster at his own game. She was up way before he had a chance to crow, bringing in a new dawn. Tuyet was up as well, already with a pot of tea cooking on the stove in the kitchen. Mom smiled gently, appreciating her thoughtfulness. Tuyet poured Mom a fresh hot cup of tea with a couple of sugar cubes, the way Mom liked it. Tuyet was a very quiet person, but her actions spoke volumes. The last few days, when Mom was preoccupied with my well-being, Tuyet quietly managed the household so well and so smoothly that no one noticed.

"Today is going to be a great day! You'll see. Hoan will get to come home today. I have a good feeling!" Tuyet told Mom, full of optimism.

Dai made his way to the kitchen. "You guys are up early! Can I have a cup of that delicious hot tea, Tuyet? We can leave in an hour or so, Mom. The hospital won't let us in early," Dai told my mom, yawning, trying to get it together. Tuyet brought him a hot cup of tea.

"We can go a little early. I want to pick up something for Hoan on the way!" Mom said gently.

"There you go again, Mom. You're going to spoil him to death," Dai said, annoyed. Mom just smiled! "I will stay in the parking lot, Mom, just in case they let Hoan go home today."

"That's a great idea. Keep our fingers crossed!" Mom said.

The hospital was quiet when Mom and Dai got there. Dai dropped Mom at the front door.

"Wait for me in the lobby, Mom. It's a little hot this morning," Dai said as he turned and drove his motorbike to the parking lot. A few minutes later, he met up with Mom, and they sat, waiting in the lobby waiting room. Not long after, Dai and Mom came up to the reception to check in, and a nurse met them in the lobby.

"How's he doing today?" Mom asked.

"He's good today. Things improved greatly since yesterday. His vitals are normal, and the doctor said there's a good chance he gets to go home today and rest at home," the nurse told them.

"Really! That's great!" Dai said.

"We still haven't figured out what caused the loss of blood and still can't find any sign of internal bleeding. It's very strange!" The nurse had a confused look on her face. "But the doctor is still working on it. For the time being, there's really nothing wrong with Hoan," she said with confidence.

"We will wait here for you. Hopefully, when the doctor comes in, we'll have good news," Dai said. Mom was excited but said nothing.

"I will let you know. Visiting hours start in thirty minutes. You can come up and see him if you want!" the nurse told them as she turned and walked away to tend to other patients. Dai gave Mom a "that's wonderful news" hug. They stood in the lobby waiting room, taking in the moment.

They made their way to my room, trying to be as quiet as they could. Mom came over to me, put her lips on my forehead, taking the "mom" temperature check, and nodded with satisfaction. Why does every mom do that? I often wondered. It is the automatic action whenever their children are sick. Not that I had any objection or anything, just wondering. Mom sat in the same chair as the previous days, Dai swinging to the other side. He smiled broadly. He had a beautiful smile, so I heard from all his dates.

"How are you feeling today, troublemaker?" Dai said, a hint of joy in his voice as if he knew something.

"I am doing fine. Did the doctor say anything about what's wrong with me?" I quizzed Mom and Dai.

"They said you are fine. There's nothing wrong with you except…" Dai let the last word lingered.

"Except what?" I said anxiously. Remember, I was only five.

"Except, you're suffering from pestidis!" Dai said, his facial expression serious.

"What's that? It sounds bad," I said, worried.

"Stop it," Mom said with a gentle smile. "You're fine, son. Nothing's wrong. They are finalizing the test results, and you can go home today.

I smiled innocently and gave Dai an "I will get you back" look.

"Stop being a pest all the time is the diagnosis and cure for what's going on with you," Dai said.

I knew he was right, but I got to take advantage of my cute face at five as much as I could. I sat up straight with anticipation.

"Did they tell you when I can go home today?" I asked, excited.

"Soon, son. The doctor will stop by in a few minutes to give us the final results and some instructions. You probably have to take medication for the few days just as a precaution." Mom gave me the details.

"As long as I get to go home. I don't like it here. It smells like medicine all the time!" I told Mom, making a "yucky" face.

"I know, son! Soon!" Mom said with relief in her voice.

The doctor walked in and broke up our conversation. "Everything looks fine, Mrs. Vu. Hoan can go home, and I will give you a prescription for some gut medicine. Have him take it twice a day for the next seven days to control his stomach acid. Try and stay bland with his diet the next few days to settle his gut down. If anything changes, call me! I will complete the discharge papers, and you can go in the next thirty minutes," the doctor told Mom, who couldn't control her happiness.

"Thank you, doctor, for taking good care of him," Mom said. Gratitude filled her answer.

I took in as much air as I could in one breath! "Freedom at last!" I screamed out loud.

"Dai, you go home. Call a taxi, and I will take Hoan home."

"Yes, Mom. You want me to get anything on my way home?" Dai asked.

"No, son. I will meet you at home!"

The taxi came to the front door of the hospital. Thinking back about this experience, as Mom and Tuyet told me, I had a second chance at life and determined to make the best of the opportunity. I thought of this story often as I was growing up. Every time, my dad's words ring true, "Violence never solves any problem. Life is valuable. Seek a peaceful solution, etc." I was glad to finally get home. The sky seemed much bluer, the air much fresher, the streets much busier.

I turned to my mom and gave her a big smile and hug. "Thank you, Mom!"

She just smiled, one of her patented picturesque smiles as I saw them often in photographs! Life was beautifully simple, and I loved every minute of it. This was our life!

Life rolled on peacefully for our family, despite the daily update of the destruction of the ongoing war on the news in nearby cities and villages. Saigon was relatively quiet and normal, if we could call it that. The cost of living rose drastically as the war dragged on. Foodstuff became scarce, and the black market thrived with illegal price gouging. But with the government too busy managing the war, many crimes went undetected and unpunished. Mom decided to open up a small bookshop to see if we could have extra income to keep up with the rising cost. With growing children and other expenses, Tuyet took over all the household responsibilities so Mom could run the bookshop. Mom was an independent woman anyway, and this gave her some time to herself outside of the home. She set up a very small bookshop. It was really a book stand at Ben Thanh Market, the busiest and most well-known market both for locals and tourists.

I was twelve and came to help Mom after school every day. The streets of Saigon were crowded around Ben Thanh Market, mostly with motorbikes and some automobiles mixed in. I loved coming to Ben Thanh Market just to watch different people walking, bargaining for stuff, and the noise was unbelievable. They got everything at Ben Thanh Market—souvenirs, fruits, vegetables, fish and meat stuff, teas, and coffees. You name it; they got it.

Mom's book stand was in one of the busiest aisles at Ben Thanh Market, and the foot traffic around the book stand helped draw a lot of looks at Mom's books. My job was to look for book peddlers (people who have old books, magazines, etc. they want to get rid of and sell them in bundles around the market) and buy books for our stand. We primarily looked for magazines since they were more popular among the tourists. One of the more popular items was *Playboy* magazine. These were really selling with the soldiers, both Vietnamese and American, who were in Vietnam, helping with the war effort. Obviously, as a kid, all I knew was the name of the magazine, and I was told to buy them to resell. Mom explicitly told me not to open up the *Playboy* magazine under any circumstances. As curious as I was by nature, I listened and obeyed Mom's direction. I loved this time of my life, spending a lot of time with Mom, feeling very useful in a small way.

Mom would let me sit next to her and call out to people walking by, asking them to stop and look at our stuff. I learned a little English during this time, just enough to say "hello, how are you" and "You buy?" holding up our magazines, books, etc. to passersby.

When we were not busy, Mom would take time to tell me stories about my grandparents, both maternal and paternal, who passed before I was born. One of my regrets was never getting a chance to know who my grandparents were. Mom knew this and would often tell me stories of the old days, growing up and dating Dad, and our grandparents.

One day, Mom told me stories about how, at first, her parents did not like Dad when he first dated her. Dad was sixteen, and Mom was seventeen. She said they thought he was too young for her and not as mature. Mom said she knew Dad was the one when she met him. He was the quiet type but very charming and charismatic. They were happy and grew more serious after several dates. A date in those days was mainly taking a walk by the countryside, relaxing on the lake, maybe the occasional hand holding. Vietnamese culture in those days was very traditional—no physical contact of any kind between a boy and a girl before they married. Mom's parents were skeptical and very strict but did not stop them from dating. In this way, Mom and Dad were very different from the expected social norms in Vietnam at that time; the year was 1946. Boys and girls rarely dated on their own; their marriages are often arranged by their families. Most parents forbade their children from dating, except when they arranged it. Thinking back, I was so proud of Mom and Dad, pioneers in their own way and ahead of the social equality curve.

Mom told me how Dad came over to pick her up for a date, riding on his old bicycle even though his family was above average. He was a man of simple tastes, not chasing after material wealth. But he was a man of strong principles and would fight to the end if he thought he was defending justice. Mom said he was quiet, even when he was young. When he got to the house, he was greeted by Mom's parents.

"Hello, Mr. and Mrs. Vu. How are you doing today?"

"We're fine, son. You know we don't much care for what you two are doing!" Mr. Vu said with disapproval.

"Sir, I like your daughter, and we're just getting to know each other. I promise you I will treat her with the utmost respect," Dad answered.

"Well, we don't like it. We love our daughter, and she wants to give you a chance. Why, we don't know," Mr. Vu told Dad.

Mom came out to meet Dad. Her parents' eyes were fixed on her and Dad. "I am ready. We can go now," Mom said.

"Mr. and Mrs. Vu, very nice meeting you, and I will have her back home soon. Thank you for letting her go with me," Dad said, as polite as ever.

Mom said his courtesy, charm, and great smile won my grandparents over after a little while, and the rest was history as the saying went! I always smiled with satisfaction and happiness whenever she told me this part of the story, and she told me this story at my request several times! Now all grown-up, I could tell where my "rebel" streak came from, and it gave me a warm feeling every time.

But Mom, too, passed away too soon, when I was in my early thirties. After a long bout with different diseases, complicated by diabetes, and being bedridden for several years, Mom joined Dad in 1996, peacefully, at my oldest sister Tuyet's home in Houston, Texas. Throughout this difficult time, Tuyet would be the one taking care of my mom's every physical and emotional need. She made the ultimate sacrifice! While taking care of her own children, she did all she could to make Mom feel as comfortable as possible during her final days! I was thankful, knowing Mom would not have to suffer any longer, and my admiration for Tuyet only grew with time. I miss Mom!

CHAPTER 5

My Favorite Sibling, Dai

Dai

Dai was gentle, handsome, and funny, as all the ladies he dated said. Dai was eleven years older than me, and we always had a special bond between us. He was not into school in the traditional sense. He had a gift when it came to the arts, teaching himself to play the guitar and getting pretty good at it. He painted stuff well too, sometimes of actual things in front of him, sometimes from his imaginative mind. He let his feeling go completely whenever he played the guitar or painted a scene, as if he were part of the song, part of a painting.

Dai attended an independent art school, not for any kind of degree but to satisfy his passion for the arts. He learned the guitar mostly on his own—listening to other people play, asking lots of questions, and buying guitar music books—and just played until his fingers bled. He had a very nice voice too and sang while he played. But socially, Dai was a little shy. He started flirting and picking up dates with girls when he was fourteen, he told me. I could not imagine myself doing that. Fourteen sounded like an awkward age to start with, and maybe a lot of "firsts" happen as people get into the early stages of adulthood, much less complicating it with flirting with girls. But that was Dai, charming, charismatic, and maybe he got a little "rebel" streak in him from Dad.

Mom told me later that Dai used to take me along with him to meet girls. She said, at five and six, I was cute, and that was his ticket in with the ladies. I vaguely remember some of the dates I was on with him, but Mom filled in some details. She said the girls he dated fell for the "Aww... He's so cool, taking care of his younger brother and babysitting him even when he's on a date!" routine. I was so young and naive; I did not know I was being used for romantic purposes. At first, I went along on these dates without asking for any fair compensation. As I got a little wiser, I started naming my conditions and Dai knew his gig was up and he had no choice but to give in to my demands. My enterprise of getting free stuff had begun, and it flourished as Dai got more involved with the ladies.

I remember one particular date. I was six at the time; Dai was in his late seventeens. He got a little more serious with a young lady he was seeing for a little while. He even brought her home to meet Mom and Dad later. Did I mention he was seventeen at the time? But the Vietnamese culture of marrying young was the norm, and Dai was no exception. The year was 1967.

"Hey, Hoan, you want to go out with me today?" Dai approached me.

"On one of your dates?" I asked.

"How do you know?" He smiled his broad, beautiful smile!

I loved his sense of self. He was full of life. He knew exactly what he wanted to do and never apologized for it, even though it sometimes upset our mom and dad. But here was where Mom and Dad broke another social norm: they allowed us kids to pursue the life we wanted, and that was very rare in the Vietnamese culture at that time, for any culture, I would guess. Dai knew he was not good at traditional school stuff—the math books, the science projects. He knew his mind did not work in that way. He was always more comfortable with the abstracts, something more imaginary, something less structured, something less logical. But in return, he was one of the most passionate and compassionate people I had ever known. There was never a time when he met people in need that he did not reach out to help. He was the emotional support person for our family, always with a big heart, big smile, big soul. He told me once, "I sometimes feel I don't belong in this world. It's too practical, too visible." I knew then he was one of a kind, that there would never be anyone like him. His mind worked differently than anyone I knew at the time. Thinking back, I had never seen him upset or mad, even when the situation was tense. He would have the smile that helped people settle their differences calmly. Later in my life, I definitely saw some of him in me.

"Maybe!" I answered Dai with a mischievous smile.

"Maybe? You never say maybe!" Dai was confused.

"Well, maybe you can take me some place before we actually go on one of your dates?" I said, hoping.

"Ah! I see where this is going!" he said with a big grin. "Okay, where do you want to go!"

"Can we go to the smoothie place I like, to start?" I asked

"To start!" He smiled again, nodding his head in agreement. "Then?"

"Uhm… maybe to the bakery you bought the birthday cake for Mom before. They have a lot of good stuff," I told him.

"Anything else, Hoan?" he said, still smiling. He knew his gig of using me to impress his dates was up. That was when I realized he really liked this particular person, the way he easily and willingly gave in to my demands. I was happy to get what I wanted in exchange for going on some of his dates. Not that I did not have it good, even on the actual dates, but if I could get something, I should, right? I felt bad later, but Dai had it coming.

But this young lady was different. Dai was serious about her. He was thinking of the *M* word, and I was obviously too young to understand why he would even consider such a thing at his age. He seemed happier, fuller at life than he usually was. He smiled much more, which was difficult to do since he smiled a lot already! He finally did it! He brought her home and introduced her to Mom and Dad! Mom was glad he found someone to at least think of settling down with. Dad was happy as well but thought it was too soon for him. Her name was Nga, a soft-spoken, sweet young lady. She was quiet and usually did not start a conversation unless being spoken to. Mom and Dad seemed to like her when they first met. Dai acted like a silly kid around her, blushing and gushing. It was very silly, even to me. Shortly after Dai brought Nga to meet Mom and Dad, tragedy struck our family.

I remember lying on my wooden bed, looking up at the ceiling. I never realized it could form interesting patterns from the natural cracks in the plaster. I felt a little tired and tried hard to close my eyes for a few minutes. I fell asleep almost instantly. The room was dark, warm, and peaceful. I felt something touching my shoulder. I looked up at a figure I could not recognize, smiling at me. I wanted to speak but couldn't. I felt my eyes growing heavy as I fell back into a deep sleep. I woke up, and the room was dark. I couldn't tell what time it was, but I imagined it to be early evening. It was almost time for dinner.

On Saturday, our family gathered for dinner. We were waiting for Dai, who still had not gotten home. My mom and my sisters were getting dinner ready. My dad was reading the newspaper. It was a typical family dinner night, and I loved it. It was getting closer to seven o'clock in the evening and no sign of Dai.

Mom began to worry. She came to my dad. "Should we call the police?"

"He's okay," my dad responded calmly.

Mom started pacing noticeably in the living room. There was a knock at the door, and my mom started to smile. "Finally!" she said. Slowly, she moved toward the door and opened it gently.

Her face fell with disappointment and fear. It was not Dai but a police officer.

"Are you Mrs. Tran?" he asked softly.

"Yes, I am!" my mom answered, her voice visibly shaky.

"I am so sorry to inform you that…" he said, his voice trailing, as my mom broke down into a devastating cry before he finished his sentence. My dad; Huynh, my oldest brother; my sisters; and I all rushed to the door. The officer was holding up my mom as she turned and fell into my dad's arms. She knew. My dad knew. We all knew.

I left everyone and headed to my comfort zone, curling myself up in a corner by the kitchen, unable to comprehend what just happened

It couldn't be, I kept telling myself.

I put my head between my knees as I felt my body rocking back and forth uncontrollably. I felt tightness in my chest. I couldn't breathe. My brother Dai and I were very close.

"He took me on a date just last week," I whispered to myself.

The vision of Dai came rushing through my head, all the dates we were on together! All the ladies he dated loved kids, and so it wasn't out of kindness that he took me along (although he cared for me a great deal). I remember usually breaking the ice on every date. My cheeks always hurt when I got home from each outing with Dai, with his dates pinching me repeatedly. He was a very popular guy, and everyone loved him. He was a very kind and genuine person. He always offered to help when he could. He had that James Dean look that made him very popular, especially in the culture in the 1960s. He was carefree and without worries. Mom and Dad did not see him a lot around the house because he always hung out with his friends and me, at least when he was on dates.

Mom was still in a state of shock. Her body shook uncontrollably as tears streamed down her face. Dad helped her to the chair in the living room. He held her tight, trying to control his own grief. I still couldn't understand it, but as devastated as I was, tears failed to come. I felt a strange sense of betrayal flush through me. Everyone expected me to cry the most out of everyone in the family. For a long time, I thought I was incapable of emotions or compassion. My own brother! How could I not have cried? Not even a single tear! No one, though, could ever understand the overwhelming grief deep inside my soul. I guess if you judged the degree of grief by the amount of tears a person shed, I would have been a zero. Mom slowly stood up and walked over to my corner. She sat down next to me and gently stroked my hair. My face, buried deep in my hands, was burning with rage. I didn't quite understand why or whom I was angry at. But I felt it!

"It's not fair!" I kept repeating myself.

"Are you okay, honey?" she spoke to me softly.

Without saying a word, I nodded lazily. Her voice still shaking, Mom pulled me close to her and just held me. Still, no tears! Maybe the shock and hurt were too much for me to feel anything but numbness. I felt a sense of tremendous loss deep within me of not just losing a big brother but someone much, much more. Although he had his faults, but he was someone I looked up to, someone with a great sense of humility and decency, carefree spirit, and compassion. Dad felt Dai was somehow lost and in the process of discovering himself, and he allowed him the freedom for him to do it. He was definitely an explorer of life. I knew he struggled at times to find himself. He was generous and good-natured. He did not seem to care much about what tomorrow would bring. He lived for today! That was one of his greatest struggles. But he wouldn't have to worry about that anymore. Maybe that was the reason why I could not cry! because in a way, he was now at peace with himself, happy wherever he was.

RIP, my dear, sweet brother! I whispered silently to myself, closing my eyes tightly.

Eighteen was just too young and too soon to be taken away from this world! The darkness in the room mirrored my soul.

Too soon, too soon! I told myself.

I miss Dai!

CHAPTER 6

My Most Admired Sibling

Tuyet

T uyet was the third child in our family but the oldest girl. She was born prematurely at seven months, living through some early medical difficulties at birth and for the next couple of years of her life! She was born with a condition known as albinism, where a person was born with very light skin due to the lack of normal skin pigmentation called melanin.

The Geneva Convention in 1954 divided Vietnam into two halves. All citizens in North Vietnam were given options to either stay where they were or move south. Tuyet was roughly two years old when our parents made the long journey south in 1954 to start a brand-new life, with all the anxiety of the uncertainties but also the excitement of a new way of life. During the 1950s, albinism was looked upon as a *curse* to a family just as *mental illness* was. Our family was very strong and never really cared about public opinion on any subject. To me, my sister Tuyet was the ultimate model sister and daughter, and any family should be so lucky to have her. I always felt a strong emotional connection to Tuyet besides the fact that she was mainly the person taking care of me growing up, anything from changing me, feeding me, or playing with me. While she rarely ever complained, I always knew she thought about the what-ifs just like anyone else would. But she kept that part of her feelings buried deep inside her. Anyone who ever met or interacted with Tuyet always felt a strong sense of confidence and contentment; she was always with a smile on her face.

Tuyet was the caretaker of the family. She was responsible for all the cooking (along with our mom) for the entire family, day in, day out. Despite some physical challenges, she never complained and was always full of energy. With albinism, she suffered from extremely poor eyesight due to the nature of this condition. Even big things in front of her looked *blurry,* and at the time, no adequate treatments, including eyewear, were developed enough to help her. But she kept on going, living as normal a life as she could, taking care of our family's everyday needs. She would grow up to be a very independent, strong woman. While I didn't tell her, I always had the highest admiration for what she did but more so her spirit—her independent, strong-willed personality. It would serve her well later when she made it to America and raised her own family, a story for another time!

I remember growing up, getting into more troubles than any child should. Tuyet was always the one to cover for me besides our mom. On the occasion when I disobeyed Dad and played soccer with friends in the front yard, knocking and breaking some valuable plants and attempting to cover up the "crime" with my homemade fixes, holding them up, Tuyet was the one who would come to my defense, although admitting the fact that I broke the rules.

"Dad, I know he broke the rules, but I don't think he did it intentionally. Boys will be boys, and he was really having a fun time with his friends. Maybe you can go easy on him a little. He deserved punishment, for sure, but maybe not so severe!"

While Dad didn't say it often enough either, but he always appreciated Tuyet's commitment to our family, and she was really good at taking care of us. Dad was always busy with *war* stuff, and whenever he was home, he was exhausted and mentally and emotionally drained from the reality of the destructive situation we were in. He found peace whenever he was home, and Tuyet was a big part of that peaceful atmosphere, along with Mom. So if anyone could somewhat persuade Dad, it would be Tuyet, and I knew it! I smiled out of one corner of my mouth as I gave Tuyet a thankful glance. Dad nodded, without saying a word, as Tuyet left the room.

"So you admit you broke the rules we talked about many times!" Dad said very softly

"Yes, sir. I did," I answered, voice shaking.

"Well, what your sister said does make some sense, but obviously, you need to learn to respect what the rules are and, more importantly, what we agreed upon. You got to honor your words, son. When everything else is no more, your words and honor are the only things you have left. So honor your words whether the times are good or when they are bad, understand?" he told me, not even a hint of anger in his voice. But I sensed a tinge of disappointment, making it even worse.

"This time, go to your room and think about what you did. You can forget about dinner and go straight to your room." He gave his final punishment.

"Yes, sir, and thank you! I will take time to think about what I did," I told him, and I stepped out of the room to head to my room, which was shared with several of my siblings.

"Are you okay?" Tuyet would ask me on the way.

"Yes, and thank you for helping me. I got off easy, just no dinner and straight to my room," I said as she nodded.

Tuyet, along with Mom, would later sneak some food up to my room. I later found out that Dad knew but kept it to himself. He always knew Mom and Tuyet would not let me go hungry the whole night. Mom and Tuyet knew as well that Dad almost expected them to do that after. I would take advantage of that "taking pity on me" feeling Mom and Tuyet had and push the rules and boundaries a few more times during my "modeled" childhood.

Tuyet was always a quiet and reserved person. She didn't show her emotions often and always spoke softly, not getting angry often, if at all. She was always aware of the situation for every occasion in our family and, more than often, became the arbiter of many disagreements and disputes among family members, with the exception of Mom and Dad. She was our voice of reason, our calm among the chaos, our excitement among the disappointments, our hope among the despair, our sensible among the irrational. I always had and continue to admire Tuyet, not for what she had done but for who she is to this day, a very strong, independent, and sensible lady who raised a full family pretty much on her own for many years without complaints.

When Mom was suffering from her illness, confined to a hospital bed at home, Tuyet was the one who single-handedly took care of her every physical and emotional need, 24-7, putting in long hours, while raising her three sons. Again it is a story for another time! The "giving it her all" attitude and personality made it easier for the rest of us, me more specifically, the chance to live our lives, do our work, and visit Mom whenever we were able. She was the ultimate *rock* of the family when we settled in America, experiencing many obstacles along the way. She asked for nothing in return.

"Live the right way! Be a good person!" she would tell us. "Go forth and *be* a *good person*!

CHAPTER 7

Me

Me!

I was your typical kid, growing up in a war-torn country with family and friends. I was the ultimate optimist, seeing the silver lining in every situation, no matter how desperate it might seem. I always assumed people were born good and good deep down when they grew up. I gave everyone the benefit of the doubt in all situations, until proven wrong. I could talk to anyone and everyone, even people I do not know. That is my nature! I am Hoan Tran, and this is my story! One of the biggest events I could recall vividly was my transition from grade school to high school. And, boy, was it dramatic!

I was twelve and starting a new chapter of my life in sixth grade, the start of high school in Vietnam. I passed the necessary exams and was admitted to one of the good public high schools in Saigon. I was both excited and scared at the same time. My family was proud of me. One of the ways to get a decent education in Vietnam was to be admitted to a good public high school (strange as it may seem compared to the United States!). The cost of private education was certainly very high, and the alternative was to study hard and pass the exams at one of the good government-subsidized high schools. My life was about to change drastically. Leaving good friends I had known since kindergarten except for a couple, I began my journey at a new and strange school with all new students, teachers, and problems. I felt butterflies in my stomach just thinking about it. But at the same time, I was very excited about things to come—new adventures, new challenges. I was known to be very stubborn, as Mom and Dad said. I was determined to be tough and face all possible new challenges head-on.

I was a tiny, skinny kid at twelve, even for Vietnamese standards. I was on the *puny* side to be exact! But I possessed a sense of confidence, or was it fear? I couldn't tell at the time! It could have been ignorance too. "You don't know what you don't know!" I took the changes in stride. After all the family customary congratulations, celebrations, hugs, and kisses, a new life began in earnest for me as reality set in. I forced myself to sleep, despite severe panic and anxiety, and tried to get ready for the first day of high school.

All the strange faces—some of them I imagined were just as frightened as I was—some of them acted tough, but I could see through their facade. They were praying that students in higher grades would leave them alone and not give them a hard time, just like I was. Some exuded a false sense of self-confidence as they hurried through the busy play yard in front of the school. I walked through quickly, trying to find my classroom without looking at anyone. In Vietnam, the teachers moved from room to room each class period, not the students. Once a student was assigned a homeroom, it would be for the whole school year. So finding the best, premium seat was a top priority! I frantically looked for classroom 6B. The number in the room indicated the grade you were in, and the letter indicated the *course of study* you signed up for. The *A* was for those students who wanted to pursue a course of study in literature. The *B* designation indicated those students who were interested in a course of study in mathematics. And the *C* was for those who were interested in general science. In my case, the 6B not only indicated an interest in mathematics but also with the selected second language focus in French. Why French? I had no idea. At twelve, I thought French was more appealing and romantic, though it was considered impractical since most parents wanted their children to learn English with the hope of winning a scholarship to study abroad in America. But I was an odd child to start with anyway. After considerable effort, I finally found room 6B.

I walked into the classroom. Many other students were already fighting for the "premium" back seats away from the teachers. We were all in uniforms, white shirts tucked inside blue khaki pants, hair neatly combed. I could see the excitement and anxiety in their eyes. They couldn't wait to get started. I had to settle for a lousy seat in the front of the room since all the "prime" back seats were taken by the early birds. They all stared at me with a mocking smile. The room was divided into two sides, with five rows of long tables and bench seats on each side, a total of ten tables. Each row seated six students for a total capacity of sixty students in each classroom. My room was packed! I put my books on the table and scanned the room. Everyone was too busy trying not to look at anyone. I smiled secretly, realizing I was finally on my way to the next stage of my life!

The class came to order as the first teacher of the day walked in. He was a medium-built man with a slight mustache, Mr. Nghiem. I thought the mustache looked funny on him but decided to keep it to myself. He had a very heavy *central region* accent (this is probably the most difficult accent to understand in the Vietnamese language!), and it was very difficult for me to understand what he was saying. But listening to the reasonable voice in my head, I kept it to myself. He took roll and began telling us what he expected of us for the school year. Obviously, I was not pleased since he was our French teacher. With that heavy central Vietnamese region accent, I could barely understand him when he spoke Vietnamese, much less French. I was obviously trying to find any reason not to like this teacher from the start. The rules he laid out were very strict, even by the strictest standards. I knew I was no longer in grade school. His rationale for these rules was he wanted us to be the best we could be.

A classic cliché, I thought.

And so the day went on.

As the first day of class went on, we had a class meeting with our class sponsor, who happened to be the literature teacher. She was very elegant and had a pleasant way about her, the complete opposite of Mr. Nghiem. She never seemed to raise her voice but always got her point across. As the sponsor of our class, she was responsible for putting this particular meeting together to select the class president for the year. Miss Lan designed an elaborate academic contest consisting not only of multiple subject matters to be studied during the school year but also everyday life challenges to see how we approached solving them, all situational stuff. She was particularly interested in the potential leadership qualities of each student and expressed her thoughts clearly to the class. She first asked any students who were interested in running for class president to volunteer. There were three students, two boys and one girl, who put their names in the hat to be considered. I didn't want to be part of this charade. Suddenly, she announced that she would like to have at least five students taking part in the process, and somehow, I was the "lucky" boy chosen along with another girl. I was stunned and started to protest, but she put an end to that quickly.

Why me? I asked myself.

I gave Miss Lan a pleading look, but she totally ignored me, officially getting the contest started.

Through the academic portion of the contest, I ended up second out of five and in contention still for class president. I blew a few answers intentionally to see if I could end up getting out of the contest, but I guess the others were doing a much better job of that themselves. The two boys and one girl who put their names in gave me a "there is no chance in hell you are going to get this class president thing!" cold stare. The second part of the contest involved questions to assess the leadership and common sense of each candidate in solving problems. The questions were all situational, and I liked them for some reason, forgetting at that moment I was deliberately trying to lose. I had a knack for dealing with abstracts and ambiguity more effectively.

"There is no right or wrong answer during this part!" Miss Lan told everyone. "So answer honestly as to how you actually deal with these situations, not how you are expected to deal with these situations. I have a way of telling when you are not completely honest!" She gave a soft smile, but the warning was there!

Miss Lan would decide after all answers were given and points were assigned to each answer in writing. She told us she would announce the final total points after the entire portion was completed. After the contest ended, we all took a half-hour break while Miss Lan tallied up the scores and decided the fate of the next class president. We took the chance, as kids do, to start talking to our neighbors while Miss Lan was occupied with the task at hand.

The boy sitting next to me was quiet and shy! "What's your name?" I asked, not a hint of shyness in my voice!

"Diep," he answered crisply. "And this is my brother, Nhat!" He pointed to the boy next to him. "We're twins!"

They did not look that alike to be twins, but he should know!

"I'm Hoan. Nice to meet you, guys! You live close to here?" I asked with a "let's be friends" smile.

"Not too far. Maybe a ten-minute bike ride!" Nhat chimed in.

"Cool! I'm about fifteen minutes from here!" I told the boys.

"What do you think of Mr. Nghiem?" Diep asked. I did not know whether to be really honest or to say the "right" thing.

"I guess he's okay. I have a really hard time understanding what he's saying most of the time," I said with a confused expression.

"We have the same problem," Nhat said. "Let's agree to help each other out this year. What do you think?

I nodded in agreement, and somehow at the pit of my stomach, I had a feeling we were going to be the best of friends.

After thirty minutes, Miss Lan called the class back in order as she was ready to announce our next class president. "I have the final scores of the contest and will announce your next class president. But before I do, I just want to tell you I am very impressed with your intelligence, common sense, and humility. Also, whoever is the next class president will have the opportunity to pick his vice president, head of arts and music, head of athletics, and head of homeroom security. The class president will have two weeks to complete these selections, so he or she has the opportunity to get to know some of the classmates before making the picks. Any questions?" Miss Lan finished with one of her patented smiles.

The whole class went very quiet and hung on to each of her words. I turned around and scanned the room. Most of the kids were taller and bigger than me. I must be one of the very few very small kids in the class. Some smiled at me, some were completely expressionless, and some just looked down at the space in front of them as we all waited for the announcement. It seemed much longer, but it was only a few minutes before Miss Lan made the pick official.

"Please don't let it be me. Don't let it be me!" I whispered under my breath, head on the table, praying very hard.

"After adding up all the scores of both the academic portion and the problem-solving, leadership portion of the contest, I present to you your next class president, Hoan Tran," Miss Lan announced excitedly.

Diep and Nhat smiled broadly and gave me hard slaps on my shoulder. I just sat there, stunned for what seemed to be forever, before Miss Lan's voice woke me out of my shock. "Come on up here, Hoan, and introduce yourself to your class! Mr. President," she said, clearly having a lot of fun at my expense.

This is not happening! Who would want the troubles and headaches? I thought to myself in total disbelief.

"Get up there!" both Nhat and Diep told me in unison. I finally unglued myself out of my seat and headed up in front of the class.

"Uh...uh... My name is Hoan. Nice meeting you all. I am looking forward to getting to know all of you and soon! Thank you!" I told the class.

Applause broke out after a few seconds of awkward silence. I let out a huge sigh of relief in my head!

Well, there you go, Hoan. Your worst nightmare came true—strange school, strange people, and you are now in charge of a group of rowdy kids. Way to go! You can't just let yourself loose, can you? I cursed myself as I walked back to my seat.

Miss Lan seemed to know my hesitance and called after me. "Hoan, you will be fine. You will do a good job. I know it!" She smiled at me. While it did not calm all my fears and anxiety, it certainly helped.

I sat back in my seat. Nhat and Diep still could not stop smiling. "Way to go, Hoan! You're da man!"

I gave them a really nasty "shut up already" look. I went through the rest of Miss Lan's class half-heartedly, trying to recover from the shock. Luckily, it was the first day, and there was not much to do.

We went through the rest of the day, meeting the remaining two teachers. As sixth graders, our classes started at one o'clock in the afternoon and went until five thirty, with a thirty-minute recess. We had a total of four teachers; each had one hour with us. Miss Lan had us for literature; Mr. Nghiem had us for French. We met our next teacher, Mr. Giao, our math and science teacher. He was a tall and heavyset man with a booming voice.

"Good afternoon, class. My name is Mr. Giao, and I will be your math and science teacher for the year! Since you are in 6B, you should be the students who have a particular liking to math and science to some extent. So I expect us to have a really productive year this year. I want you to pay attention. Ask as many questions as you need to understand everything we learn. Don't be afraid of asking a dumb question. The only dumb questions are those that are not asked, and you end up confused and not learning all that you should. Any questions?" Mr. Giao looked around the room. "By now, you should have picked your class president. So would the class president kindly stand up and take roll for me?" he continued.

"Yes sir. My name is Hoan, and I am the class president," I told Mr. Giao as I walked up to his desk to take the sheet of paper he gave me with the names of all the students in the class.

"Hoan, my expectation is for you to make sure the class is in order prior to the start of each of my class. I will hold you responsible if there is no order during any one of my classes. Understood?" he told me before I headed back to my seat.

"Yes sir! Understood!" I answered, heading back and sitting down next to Diep. There was a look of worry in his eyes, knowing now it would be a big challenge to keep this rowdy group in check. If anyone wanted to make trouble for me, it would not be difficult to do that by starting a ruckus of some kind during any of the four classes we had, not just Mr. Giao's. I nodded at Diep and Nhat, with the "I know, I know" look.

The last teacher we met that day was Miss. Kim, our history teacher. She was tall and slender, in her early thirties. She was soft-spoken but sounded very firm with every word.

She started talking to us, "We will study both Vietnam and world history in this class. My goal is for you to expand your knowledge of the world we live in. In order to build the future, we must understand our history and how to improve upon it and grow. My hope is you will pay attention and learn as much as you can. I know you are in 6B, and the focus is on mathematics, but there is more to life than numbers and equations. Would the class president please come up and take roll for this class." She looked down at the crowded room, waiting.

"Yes, ma'am. I am Hoan and the class president for this year!" I said, again walking up to the front. This whole "class president" thing was already getting tiresome. I made several trips to the front, and it was only our first day of school. I tried to hide my frustration. I rattled off the names since it was the third time I had done it that day.

Ms. Kim called after me as I headed back to my seat, and I knew what she was going to say. "Hoan, make sure you keep your class in order at the start of my class. Everyone should be in their seats and ready to go prior to you taking roll. Is that clear?" she said softly, but I could feel the steeliness in her voice.

"Yes, ma'am. I will," I answered quickly and headed back to my seat.

I survived my first day in high school. Throwing my books on the floor, I settled myself on my wooden bed the minute I got home, closing my eyes for a few minutes. I knew I had to tell my whole family everything at dinner as we normally would. But tonight will be a little different, with my whole family full of anticipation about my first day in high school. I fell asleep until there was a knock on my door.

"Hoan, get ready for dinner. We eat in fifteen minutes," Tuyet, my oldest sister, said to me through the closed door.

"I will be right there!" I said, my voice heavy and tired.

I quickly got out of bed, changed out of my school uniform into shorts and a T-shirt, and headed to the dining room, still groggy from the quick nap. "Here we go!" I whispered to myself, putting on a smile as I walked.

I could tell everyone was dying of anticipation. While Mom and Dad were cool about letting us kids be who we were and pursue whatever life we chose, always providing support and good old-fashioned teachings, they were extremely tight about how we handled each situation in life, big or small. So were my siblings. It was one of their very few flaws I could see. I sat in my usual seat at the dining table. The food smelled great this evening, but somehow, my appetite was not up to it, still reeling from the shock of being selected class president this very eventful day. We all waited for Mom and Dad to pick up their chopsticks to start dinner. In Vietnam, no one ate until the parents commence dinner by picking up their chopsticks. Then we waited one by one, from the oldest to the youngest siblings, to pick up the chopsticks in order. Guess where in that line I was! But I did not mind since before I could pick up my chopsticks, either Mom or my older siblings already put food in my rice bowl. It was one of the perks of being the younger sibling. Everyone began eating, and I was really hoping they would forget about our customary "tell us about your day" ritual. But to my disappointment, they did not.

"So how was your first day at school, son?" Dad started the ball rolling on the "conversation avalanche,"

"Yeah, tell us all about it!" all my siblings said in unison.

"Well, it was okay, I guess! Nothing special!" I lied.

"Well, you got to give us more than that, son! How do you feel after the first day? Different from grade school, I'm sure," Mom said gently, cuing me in on the conversation.

"Well, everyone, it was a very good day actually. Got to meet and became friends with a couple of boys. I like all the teachers so far, some more than the others," I started my portion of the "let's share our day" ritual. Everyone at the table listened with much more intense interest than I thought the conversation actually deserved.

I swallowed and continued, "It was just your basic introduction day—teachers telling us their rules and expectations like the adults they are, kids were being rowdy at times as they usually are, and I was elected class president. The end! Now who's next!" I tried to gloss over the last part quickly and moved on.

"Hold it!" Dai said. Of course, he would be the one who called me out.

I will make him pay for this, I thought to myself, giving him a very evil look. He either did not see it or totally ignored me.

"Go back to the last part again, please?"

"Kids are rowdy at times as they usually are?" I repeated.

"Ah, no, the part after that!" Dai said again with emphasis. I scratched my head as if trying to remember. "Quit stalling." Dai's voice was louder this time.

"Alright, I was elected class president! Obviously, not by choice," I said unenthusiastically.

"What do you mean not by choice, son?" Mom asked gently.

"Well, it's a new school, Mom. I don't know any of the students in that class. Well, I know two of them now but not the rest. I don't know the teachers well yet, and I don't like all the attention." It felt good letting my true feelings out, and I, unknowingly, let out a smile.

"Why should that be a problem, son?" Dad chimed in.

"Well, Dad, I want to have time to myself to study and get to know people at my pace. Being class president is a lot of responsibility, and the teachers told me I have to be responsible for making sure the class is in order throughout the day. Sixty kids, Dad! Sixty kids just starting high school. That's a lot," I said as if protesting the process. Mom and Dad smiled. I objected, "It's not funny!"

"How did you end up being class president, son? And by the way, we are all very proud of you," Mom said.

"Well, our sponsored teacher, Miss Lan, had a contest where she tested our academic, leadership, and situational problem-solving skills. And somehow, I ended up with the most points after the contest, and here we are!" I told Mom as if the process was intentionally stacked against me.

At that point, everyone broke out laughing, and I got angry and dug into my bowl of rice without looking up at anyone. They continued to laugh, maybe at how silly I was at the time. After they had their moment, we all ate, and my siblings told their stories for the day, and it went much smoother than my story did. I kept to myself, eating, with the occasional nod to my siblings' stories as if I actually heard them. Dinnertime seemed to last twice as long that day as it usually did. When it was over, I took to my room, exhausted mentally from having to relive the first day at school I was absolutely trying to forget. But on the bright side (there is always a bright side with me, no matter how terrible the situation is), I already made two very good friends I could talk to if I ran into any issues. Did I mention I was the smallest kid in my entire class?

I cursed under my breath at my luck, thinking, *It will probably get worse.*

I fell asleep from exhaustion of a very eventful day.

During class the next day, Mr. Nghiem congratulated me on being elected class president. He reminded the class of the rules as he stressed accountability. If the class did not behave appropriately (though he did not get specific about what appropriate looked like), he would not only punish the individuals causing the problems but also hold the class president responsible for not carrying out the security expectations for the entire class. I thought it was extremely unfair, given the fact that I was new and didn't even want to do it in the first place.

He got to be kidding! Getting a bunch of sixth graders to behave for the entire school year confined in a small room? What was he thinking? I felt a tinge of anxiety as the thoughts hit me. For a twelve-year-old, this was absolutely uncalled for. But after wallowing in much self-pity, I accepted my responsibility for the entire class and moved on.

I officially began a new chapter of my life, which is obviously off to a rocky start at best. So it was the beginning of my truly growing up and accepting the first real responsibility of my young life. I miss that time terribly and finally understood what Dad had been trying to teach me. It shaped me into the person I am today, and I realized it was alright not to be perfect.

So on with sixth grade! It was an awkward time for the first couple of months. All the students were trying to feel each other out, especially me. They wanted to see who I was and what to expect from me. As for me, I was just trying to survive in a new school, new people, new teachers, new classes…new everything! I tried to find a way to manage my new responsibilities as class president as well as my workload for new classes. I did make some good friends who supported me wholeheartedly, and it didn't hurt that they were much bigger than me, making me feel safer. We had all types of students in class—the quiet ones, the talkative ones, the troublemakers, etc. Each was there for a different reason.

One single event during the school year finally won me the support and respect of the entire class, and of course, it happened during Mr. Nghiem's class, the first class of the day. We were caught one day as Mr. Nghiem walked into class, finding it in total chaos: paper planes flying everywhere, erasers being thrown across the room, students getting up on the table and stomping their feet—all the usual things kids that age would do. They just wanted to get off some steam before class started, and of course, Mr. Nghiem decided to show up a few minutes early for class that day.

"Really! You are never early. You're the most on-time person I know!" I cursed under my breath.

The room went totally silent as Mr. Nghiem settled into his desk. He just stared down the class for what seemed to be an eternity. Finally, he summoned me to the front of the class. Before he lowered the hammer, he kindly reminded me of my responsibility and asked me if I still remembered.

"Yes, sir. But the class hasn't officially started yet, sir," I told him, being very honest! As expected, he was not pleased to hear that.

"Mr. Tran, what I told you was that the class has to be ready whenever I show up to start the class. And obviously, you failed to live up to your responsibility today." He was stern in his response. "Of all days, it happens to be the day we are having one of our biggest tests of the year." I cursed my luck. He promptly asked me, "Do you mind giving me the names of all the students responsible for this whole mess?"

I remember looking around the room. All the faces were tense and focused on me, waiting and hoping I would not reveal their names. In Vietnam, any disciplinary infractions would go on your school record permanently, negatively impacting students' ability to advance into the next level. I paused for a few seconds and turned back to Mr. Nghiem and said calmly (which surprised even me!), "Sir, the only name I can give you is mine!"

He looked at me, half smiling, "*You*! You are responsible for all this? Com'on now, son! Give me those names. I'll give you one last chance to tell me those names, or I will be forced to give you a zero on this exam as part of the punishment for letting this whole mess happen. If I have the names, you will be allowed to take the exam."

Again all the faces in the room stared at me intensely, waiting for my response.

After some consideration, I told Mr. Nghiem, "I can't do that, sir. As you reminded me, as class president, I am responsible for keeping my class in order, and I failed. I guess I have to get a zero for the exam. Although I just want to let you know that can easily ace this exam. I studied hard for this exam, sir, and…" I stopped midsentence and stayed silent.

Mr. Nghiem took his time and finally spoke again, "Very well! As I said, you will get a zero for this exam as part of the punishment, and we can move on." He looked at the entire class. "As for all of you, let's not make a habit of this. The next time, you are all going to be punished regardless." He turned to me again. "You can get back to your seat, son."

I could tell from the expressions on their faces that all the students were relieved, with a hint of admiration and guilt. I smiled to myself as I got back to my seat, content with getting a zero for the exam. I was confident I could make it up eventually. I finally grew up and became part of something much bigger in the process.

The next day, all my classmates flocked around me, expressing their appreciation for not giving them up the day before. The tallest and biggest boy in class (he stood roughly five feet eight inches for a sixth grader) came over and introduced himself, giving me a strong pat on the back, so strong it almost knocked me to the ground. Everyone was laughing hard as he pulled his hand back.

"Oh! Sorry about that. I got carried away! My name is Long. Good stuff yesterday. You saved our butts. From now on, we got yours!" he said, embarrassed.

"No worries and thank you. I did what I needed to do!" I smiled back. Little did I know, my friendship with Long would come in handy later as we got into some altercations with other kids at a different school.

Diep and his twin, Nhat, who later became my best friends, went out of their way to let me know how strong they thought I was for a tiny boy!

I thought, *Is that supposed to be a compliment?*

From that moment on, I learned a sense of duty, leadership, and a true appreciation for friendship. I carried that with me throughout my life, from the age of twelve to adulthood. It saved me many times when I faced challenges and adversities in my life. I also realized that lessons learned in life were not necessarily intended or planned. Life just happens, and you learn as you go along! I smiled appreciatively at Diep and Nhat and told them I hoped someday I could continue to live by the principles I had learned during my first year in high school. We walked together through the school's playground; the start of a great, long-lasting friendship began!

I thought of my dad's words circling in my mind, *All this is what Dad always taught me—living by principles and standing firm on them. Don't waver under any circumstances! Fight for what's right, not with your fists but with your compassion!*

Slowly, I realized Dad was getting me ready to grow up the right way. I smiled even broader, and Diep wondered, "Something good?" I just nodded, and we walked home!

CHAPTER 8

Parlez-Vous Francais?

The next several months went smoothly at school, especially with Mr. Nghiem, who kinda grew on me. But all of us still tried hard to understand whenever he started speaking in French, his accent being so heavy. I was working my way back from the zero I got for not keeping our class in order.

"*Bonjour*, class!" He started every class with this old goodie. "Comment allez vous tous aujourd'hui?" Hello, class. How are you all doing today?

At the beginning of the year, Mr. Nghiem warned us that he would allow us to speak Vietnamese but only for the first month, then it would be all in French, "You have to ask your questions in French, and I will answer in French. That's how you learn more quickly. So make sure you do your homework and work hard on your French-speaking skill."

So here he was, living up to his early warning. I was trying very hard to avoid getting into a conversation with Mr. Nghiem since I was not very good. Unfortunately, he did not ask for volunteers. One of his rules was all students had to be ready as he would call on us randomly throughout his class.

We all answered with one loud voice, "Nous allon bien, monsieur! Comment allez vous?" We are fine, sir. How are you?

Mr. Nghiem smiled, seemingly pleased.

He rattled off very quickly, "Aujourd'hui, nous en apprendrons advantage sur la construction de phrases afin que vous puissiez bien-

75

tot commencer a rediger un essai." Today, we will learn about sentence construction so you can start writing an essay soon!

All of us looked at each other, jaws dropping, scrambling to understand.

He continued before we had a chance to translate and understand his first sentence, "Le monde comprend?" Everyone understands?

But everyone pretended they understood and nodded lazily. He did not seem to pay attention and continued to speak what we all interpreted as "Blah, blah, blah, blah…" We saw his lips moving, and sounds were coming out of his mouth, but we barely understood any of it.

"Monsieur Tran!" I jolted myself in my seat as he called my name.

"Monsieur!" I responded reflexively.

He rattled off at a dizzying pace, "Quelles sont les parties de base d'une phrase et en quoi est-ce different en francais du vietnamien?" What are the basic parts of a sentence and how is it different in French from Vietnamese?

"Ah, ah, ah…" was all I could manage. I tried to buy some time. "Pouvez-vous s'il vous plais repeater cela, monsieur?" Can you please repeat that, sir?

He looked at me intensely. "Je sais ce que tu fais, fils." I know what you are doing, son.

"I am just trying to understand, sir!" It slipped out of me in Vietnamese, and I immediately realized the consequences.

He said sternly, "Francais seulement, Monsieur Tran!" French only, Mr. Tran.

The class held back their laughter.

Mr. Nghiem did this a lot. Somehow, he got more pleasure from making me an example to the whole class and seeing me squirm. But surprisingly, we learned quite a bit. Mr. Nghiem had his way of teaching, and slowly, we understood more and more as we were only allowed to speak only French. It forced us to pay more attention, learn how to put together a sentence quickly, and how to speak it correctly. I came to admire Mr. Nghiem's patience. Deep down, he really cared about us, even though he was always tough with us. He taught us more than French. He taught us to stick to what we believed to be right and not let others influence us and make us waver on our principles.

Mr. Nghiem shared with us, on one rare occasion, that he had two children, one boy and one girl. He talked to us about responsibility, keeping our word, and taking care of the ones we loved. For one brief moment, he was very human, expressing his inner feelings. He made me realize how important it was for me to fulfill my responsibility as class president, whether I initially wanted to or not.

"Sometimes you don't get to choose what happens in your life. But you have a choice on how to handle those things that happen. Remember, children, the choices you make not only affect you, but they also have consequences for others, good or bad. So always make your choices with compassion and thoughtfulness," he would say to all of us.

One thing unique about the Vietnamese culture then is that no matter what subject they taught us in class, all our teachers would, on occasion, teach us about life and how to grow up to be a good person and a good contributor to society. I came to love all of my teachers. They were my second parents. They truly gave themselves to teaching, taking good care of us intellectually, morally, and emotionally. I felt a sense of true blessing, especially when we were in the middle of a never-ending civil war. These were the people who made our lives more colorful, enjoyable, and inspiring.

The bell rang, and I could not have appreciated anything more.

Mr. Nghiem told our class, "Assurez-vous de lire le devoir de demain, il ya aura un petit questionnaire simple a ce sujet." Please make sure you read the assignment for tomorrow. There will be a short, simple quiz about it.

We all chimed in unison, "Oui, monsieur! Merci, monsieur!" Yes, sir. Thank you, sir.

And I let out a big sigh of relief. French was done for the day!

CHAPTER 9

"We're Going on
a Field Trip"

M r. Giao was our "grandpa" figure. He had been teaching for over forty years and loved every minute of it. He was a wizard at math and science. He was my favorite teacher and put a lot of thought into every class. He would design unique experiments for every class and make it so much fun. I was particularly appreciative because I am much more of a visual learner. If I could see it, I could remember it! Mr. Giao had the challenge of teaching both math and science, so we studied math one week and science another week and back and forth. I excelled in math and especially science. Did I mention I was a very curious boy by nature? Mr. Giao tried not to bring me up as an example to the class since he did not want to be seen as biased. But I held my own and did very well in his class.

One day, Mr. Giao announced we would be going on a field trip to the New Year's Flower Festival at Tao Dan Flower Park. It was 1973, the year of the ox. That was my birth year in the zodiac. We were on the subject of botany, learning about plants, trees, flowers, etc., and I remember how excited I was both for New Year's and the field trip. I later found out that since the school was very limited in funds, Mr. Giao sometimes had to put up his own money for us to go. That was dedication at its best. I never forgot how deeply touched I was to learn that, especially since Mr. Giao rode an old bicycle to work every day. He was my role model of compassion and genuine caring for people!

Our class with Mr. Giao started every day at two o'clock in the afternoon, but because of the field trip, we got an early start. I was already up at six o'clock that morning, getting ready for our field trip at eight. We would all meet Mr. Giao at the front of Tao Dan Garden's gate. I wondered how Mr. Giao would manage to keep sixty kids, some more rowdy than others, in line at a big flower park like Tao Dan. But if anyone could do it, it would be Mr. Giao. He towered over people and was fairly intimidating, but he had the heart of a gentle soul.

Diep and Nhat met me at my house early that morning so we could ride our bikes together to Tao Dan Park. My house was very close to the park, and for whatever reason, it was always a meeting spot whenever us kids met to go somewhere together. Mom and Dad loved Diep and Nhat like their own sons. They were polite, pleasant, very good folks, and quite orderly. I had a suspicious feeling they wished I was a little more like them and not so much of a troublemaker, getting myself into tough spots. Maybe that was why Diep, Nhat, and I got along well. We had things in common but were opposite in our approaches and personalities. They told me they loved the "rebel" in me, the "bucking the system" personality, not conformity. It was so easy for us from day one in class. We could talk to each other freely from the start. From that day on, there was no doubt in my mind that we would be the best of friends.

We made it to the front of Tao Dan Park; the early peaceful surroundings got us three excited as we waited for the others. We pulled our bikes into the parking spots and walked over to the front gates. We were a good thirty minutes early and decided to take a walk around. Vietnam was not as hot this time of year, February, making it much more pleasant if we were to walk around the park for a few hours! Vietnam stayed fairly consistently hot and humid, in the midnineties for both. As kids, though, we did not seem to mind it as much. We could play in the streets for hours, ignoring the heat and humidity by sweating our butts off.

The food vendors were already out for a few hours prior to us kids walking around. They would start selling their stuff around four o'clock in the morning for the early risers and workers. We could smell the aroma of the noodle shops. The sweet, smoked BBQ made our mouths water. The smoothie and sugar cane juice shops were very popular, with people lining up. With the heat and humidity, they kept busy every minute of every day they opened. Vietnamese money at that time had little value on the exchange, four to five hundred Vietnamese dong (our currency) for every American dollar! With American soldiers helping fight the war at that time, the dollar was in very high demand. In all the big shops at our main tourist market, Ben Thanh Market, the dollar was the most frequently used currency to buy goods.

I looked at Diep and Nhat. "You want to get some sugar cane juice? I'm kinda thirsty!"

They laughed at me caringly. "We wouldn't want you to be thirsty now, would we, sir?" They teased me a lot by the way. "Of course, we can!" they said as we walked over to a sugar cane juice shop.

We got our sugar cane juice and started heading back to Tao Dan Park. The sweetness of the sugar cane, cold and crisp, really hit the spot. We smiled with satisfaction as we stood in front of the park. Mr. Giao was already there when we got back, smiling to us.

"I see you boys already got started. You probably will need a few more of those by the time we get through today!" We nodded.

"We know, sir. We will drink very slowly!" Of course, I had to give a smart-assed answer!

The kids slowly packed the front gates of Tao Dan Park; some of them, just like us, traveled in packs. Mr. Giao, list of names in hand, had no trouble seeing all the kids, given how tall he was. He got a small bullhorn and started speaking in his booming voice. The park was expecting us, as they asked Mr. Giao to move us kids to the door to the right of the group entrance. Mr. Giao asked everyone to stand to one side, and as he called our names, we moved to the right gate to verify we were checked in. After roughly fifteen minutes, each of us was present and accounted for. Mr. Giao gave the attendant the single code he had purchased all the tickets with. She matched it against her reserved list of codes and signaled us to line up by twos. As she let us through the door, she stamped our hands just in case we needed to get in and out of the park, which we could not do since it was a group outing with Mr. Giao.

Finally, we were on the park grounds, and Mr. Giao gave us instructions, "The purpose of our field trip today is for all you children to explore what we learned in class. The plants, the trees, and the flowers each belong to a certain family. I want all of you to write down everything you can identify by its Latin name. Tomorrow, I will collect them from you and have a prize for the top three groups to get the most right! Before we do that, I will take you to a couple of spots I think are fascinating, which you should know. Then I will break you into groups of four for a total of fifteen groups. Your job is to divide and conquer. You will each explore and write down all you can individually, then combine your findings at the end of our trip. One of you needs to put together the master list for the group and submit it to me tomorrow in class! Is everyone clear on what to do?" He looked expectantly at all of us.

We nodded in unison, anxious to get started. As I hoped, Diep; Nhat; a boy named Thao, whom I selected for the security officer for the class; and I were on the same team. We high-fived each other with broad smiles, anticipating doing all we could to win. When everyone got together with their teams, Mr. Giao led the way to our first destination, the flower garden. There were flowers everywhere in so many colors, so many shapes, and they were so beautiful. Who said math and science had to be boring? We had a blast, tired but thrilled by a day well spent. Mr. Giao was right! We needed that sugar cane juice as we made our way through our competition at the park. Time went by fast, and before we knew it, the field trip was over. We headed to the front gates.

Mr. Giao gave us the last instructions, "Remember, children, put together one list per group, and I will collect them in class tomorrow. Be careful going home!"

With that, the students dispersed in all directions. Diep, Nhat, and I stayed around for a few more minutes, deciding we were hungry and would get something to eat around the park. We certainly had our choices!

What a day! I thought. *This might work out very well, after all. I am getting the hang of this high school gig now.*

In class the following day, we were excited to hear the results from the field trip and see which of the fifteen teams would take home the top three prizes.

"Alright, children. First, thank you for behaving very orderly yesterday at Tao Dan Park. I hope you all had some fun doing the assignment," he started.

We all spoke in unison, "Yes, sir! We did. Can we do another one?"

"We will see. But the idea is that hopefully you learned something and how it matched up against your textbook—some practical lessons. I have the results from yesterday's contest. They were very close, but I have the top three winners. I will start with number three and move up." Mr. Giao got the kids all excited, dragging it out a little longer before we got going with math.

To our disappointment, our team came in second. But Diep, Nhat, Thao, and I still gave each other high fives for the effort. Mr. Giao congratulated the winners and moved on to his math lessons. He knew how to get kids excited and motivated to learn. He was the more practical teacher, always giving us real-life experiences to prove a mathematical theory or to identify living things in the universe. He brought the lessons to life, literally, and we ate them up, hungry for more.

After the contest for science was settled, Mr. Giao got into our math lesson for the day. It was amazing to see how he switched from the more poetic nature of science—the beautiful flowers and majestic plants—to the drier numbers and equations. But Mr. Giao did it with ease and in such simple terms that we all could understand. With science, Mr. Giao's job encompassed all—including some chemistry, physics, and biology. He got a big job of giving us an introduction to the essential subjects of science and math in one year, a very tall order for anyone. Mr. Giao did not seem to fret about it one bit. He was patient and passionate about everything science. After forty years, he still showed excitement every time we heard him speak on these sub-jects. I appreciated the attitude of Mr. Giao, sometimes even more than the practical lessons themselves. He got us all excited about learning science and math, an excellent accomplishment!

Diep struggled with math and science, while Nhat, on the other hand, a less abstract person, seemed to be doing fine. I always won-dered how they could be twins and be so different. Diep excelled in the arts and music, while Nhat could not carry a tune if his life depended on it. Yours truly was int the middle of the road, one foot in the science and math door and the other in the arts and music door, not particularly great at either one. I learned from both Diep and Nhat quite a bit. I saw some of myself in each of them, and they carried me through some rough times in high school.

CHAPTER 10

"The World Is Your Oyster"

Ms. Kim, our history teacher, was full of energy, and we could tell she loved history with a passion. If she had the opportunity, she could talk for days about the events happening in Vietnam and around the world. She was very philosophical when it came to history.

She told us, "History shapes our future. People who fail to learn from history are setting themselves up for disappointment, and our world will fail to advance and make progress, just as we learn from our own personal mistakes and do better. That's our own personal *history*. We have to respect history, honor history, value history, and nurture history. History is our path forward to help mankind, to advance society, and to plan for the future of the world."

She would begin her first class with a very eloquent summary of history.

"We sitting here today, able to enjoy the company of one another and learn, is the result of years and years of sacrifice by our forefathers who fought to preserve our history, our heritage, and our society. We should and must remember and honor that."

I felt an urge to debate her points, not that I did not agree with her. I did! But I also had, at that time, my own perspective. I struggled with whether or not to raise my hand and share my thoughts, my perspective.

Ms. Kim sensed my anxiousness. "Mr. Tran," she called out.

"Yes, ma'am!" I responded

"You are our class president?" she asked, already knowing the answer

"Yes, ma'am!" I repeated the same answer

"I sense you have something to say. I want to make it clear to all of you that I welcome your thoughts. This is how we learn. We share and challenge each other. I only ask for one thing: if you are going to make a point, make sure you are able to back it up with logical thoughts. Now, Mr. Tran, what's on your mind?" She looked at me gently.

"Well, it's just that I agree with everything you're saying. We need to honor and learn from history and appreciate our forefathers' sacrifices. Learning from history is a valuable way to chart our path forward. When I read our own history and some world history, sometimes I disagree with the vision and the thought process of previous generations and how they approach society, conforming its people to certain social norms, making people hesitant or afraid to be themselves, and doing things in their own ways to contribute to society," I blurted out a long thought.

"Well, Mr. Tran, obviously, you have given history some thought. We will get to those things you talk about soon enough. I appreciate your willingness to share your thoughts with us," she said to me. "Now for the rest of the class, we will be getting into many different topics, discussions of history. I will reserve 20 percent of the final grade to participation and sharing your thoughts. We will have a monthly *debate* competition where you will be given a topic and will be divided into twelve teams of fives. Points will be given to each team, and I will tally the points at the end of the year and select a 'Team of History' for this class. So get ready to learn, participate, contribute, and be part of history and be part of making history." She smiled, obviously enjoying herself.

History was not my strength, but surprisingly, I enjoyed it more than I thought I would. Ms. Kim was a great teacher, using old movies and setting up reenactments of historical events in class, where we kids got to play different historical figures while working through the history lesson of the day. She would always end each lesson by asking us, "If you were the leaders in these events, would you have done anything different? And more importantly, if so, do you think it would have changed the outcome of history?" These were some thought-provoking questions and probably way too deep for a bunch of twelve-year-olds. I always had something to say, whether right or wrong. I always felt a sense of obligation as class president to lead by example, contributing my thoughts so we could have much richer conversations, especially when it came to our history and the history of the world. Ms. Kim always tried to get us to be more aware of everything around us, of things going on in the world. Back in those days, news was very limited, whether in print or on television, given that very few families could afford to have televisions. The government, while a democratic one in the south, still controlled the news—what was given for public consumption. Freedom of speech was more limited. Ms. Kim was a little more progressive than most, sharing news with us and explaining how it fit in with history or drawing parallels to history. She was very meticulous about all the details and got us involved in dissecting the details of history. Of all the teachers, she gave out the most homework, which I was not a fan of, but they were fun assignments where we could take the topic in any direction. She did not handcuff us on any specifics and allowed our imagination to take over.

At our school, the year-end art festival for the sixth graders was a big historical event, where each class got to put up a play based on a historical event or person of their choice. From all those plays, they picked one to represent the school at the year-end ceremony. Ms. Kim was our sponsor and director for the year-end play put on by our class. Diep was our arts and music officer and responsible for getting our class to agree on a topic, audition for the characters, and schedule all rehearsals. I selected him to serve in that capacity because he was a very artistic and musical person. He knew a lot about the arts and music of all genres, including international music. He was always curious about the history of the arts and music and how they evolved over the centuries. He was a very avid reader of different cultures and how arts and music shaped different cultures and countries and had an impact on their political systems of government and history. After I announced his selection, all the students voted for him unanimously. He would be the go-to person for this year-end extravaganza.

"I was thinking about our year-end play and have an idea. You want to hear it?" Diep stopped me in the play yard during recess one day.

"Really? Great. Let's hear it!" I said with anticipation.

"I was thinking of doing a play on Tran Hung Dao, one of our country's most accomplished generals and royal family member of the Tran Dynasty." He paused, waiting for my reaction.

"That's a great idea. Why don't you present them to the class during our history hour with Ms. Kim?" I told Diep. He smiled the biggest smile I had ever seen, excited and already working his imagination.

"But I have to make sure I pick certain events that would highlight his historical accomplishments. Otherwise, I can't fit everything in one play," Diep, his head already working on the details, mumbled to himself. I could not help but feel the contagious excitement.

Tran Hung Dao, indeed, was one of our most famous and respected historical heroes, conquering enemies to preserve the freedom of our country. He had a huge statue dedicated to his accomplishments at Tran Hung Dao Square in the center of Saigon, a bustling business district. But if anyone could do it, I am totally confident Diep would be able to. He got a very rich imagination and would be able to combine the arts and music into the play. And with Ms. Kim as our sponsor, I was sure we would be a tough competitor and a team to be reckoned with. With that, we turned our attention back to recess!

CHAPTER 11

"Life Is a Blank Canvas"

Miss Lan, our literature teacher, was an elegant and eloquent communicator. She spoke softly and gently to us kids, but her authority was unmistakable. Everything she said was pure poetry. She had a magnificent command of the language and literature and was a great storyteller. She, like my other three teachers, was passionate about what she taught but, more importantly, cared genuinely about her students personally. She was our class sponsor and the one who put me in the predicament I was in, albeit unintentionally. But in a way, I was glad she did. As I grew into my role as class president, I could see my transformation from a much shier kid to a more outgoing, outspoken person. I could hardly recognize myself.

Is this what my dad has in mind for how he wants me to grow and get better at? I thought to myself, smiling secretly.

Miss Lan, in her traditional Vietnamese dress (*Ao Dai*), dazzled the class every time she walked in. We were lucky that all our teachers were very dedicated and brought their subjects to life, and Miss Lan was no exception. She would show us movies, documentaries, and comic books to show us the different uses of literature and how it shaped our culture and society in general but, more importantly, as unique individuals. The way we spoke, the words we used, and the phrases we composed all made us who we were.

"Don't ever underestimate the power of your words. They are your unique voice, and you must use them when you feel there is any kind of injustice or inequity to speak up for the weak, the poor, and the less fortunate. You must use your words to build a better future for yourselves and the many more generations to come. We are where we are as a country because of our failure to use our words to solve problems and change minds. We go straight for the destruction. In this class, we will see how powerful words are and how you can use them to change the world. Poetry, novels, music, and the arts are all forms of literature, expressing thoughts and ideas that change the world. We will go to museums to explore, to plays at the community theater, and to recitals at local neighborhoods to strengthen and enrich our sense of culture and community."

Ms. Lan's voice was soft, but everyone could sense the passion and strength in her every word. She was a very powerful public speaker. In Ms. Lan, we got a very different kind of teacher. She was elegant, using her words to change lives, to undo biases, to build the community, and to shape society. She was an absolute social activist and would put herself at the front of every battle to conquer injustice and social inequality. Ms. Lan brought the community to every lesson she taught, and she made literature fun and exciting. In every book she had us read, she tried to help us explore the meaning of it and its significance to the community and society. She would have us challenge social norms, be different, and be who we wanted to be. She never held back, even when she knew the consequences were not good. She taught us to have the courage to push back and to resist injustices, and there were many in Vietnam. During wartime, her attitude resonated with the rebels in many, if not all, of us. She instilled a sense of pride and self-worth in each of us and demanded a lot from us as young men. Halfway through Ms. Lan's class that year, we accidentally grew up without realizing it. I loved coming to Ms. Lan's class every day. It felt like I was actually living life in that class.

Ms. Lan sponsored the debate club, where every month, our class's team would debate a team from a different school on literature, social issues, the war, and many other topics. This taught us to discuss, debate, and challenge the many social topics in our society, and I, again, was selected as one of the three members of our team. I just couldn't help feeling how lucky I was (that was sarcasm, by the way, if you didn't detect that!). I was a shy kid when I first started first grade, and the thought of just speaking, much less debating, in front of parents, teachers, and other students terrified me, to say the least. But as with being class president, I did not have a choice, although the selection process was free and fair. It was not as though I was coerced into it. But nonetheless, I cursed my luck in these "fair processes."

I remember the *practice session* we had in preparation for our first competition. Diep, our arts and music officer; Thao, our security officer; and I made up the debate team, which was a stroke of luck because we operate on similar wavelengths as far as our academic and social thinking. We went up against Nhat (Diep's twin) and two other classmates. The topic of the practice debate was "How Music Can Shape Society and Whether It Is Right for People to Appreciate or Hate a Certain Genre of Music." This was a dream come true for Diep, who spent his whole short life, at the ripe age of twelve, on music and the arts. Ms. Lan gave us thirty minutes to prep among our teams. We were the team selected to start the debate and present our premise to the class. While Thao and I were not as strong in music and the arts, we were fairly good at arguing a point, which was always a plus when you debated.

"Music—the power of will, the power of individuals, the power of community, the power of expression, the power of change, the power of a movement, the power of healing, the power of thoughts, the power of voice for everyone. Should I go on? Music challenges, shapes, and demands change and, at the same time, soothes, heals, and strengthens emotions. It represents not just *one voice* but *all voices*, the ultimate freedom of expression, a deep look into our souls, and a symbol of who we are or maybe what we want to become. Music unites different peoples and cultures around the world, even those that don't speak the same language, don't share the same cultures, and don't have the same degree of freedom. Music is the bridge that connects people with different degrees of suffering and hardship to come together to heal, to share a moment of tranquility, to express a moment of appreciation. Music of all genres shares a common bond: it *unites* people and *commands thoughts*!" Diep started the debate with a very elegant and powerful opening.

Thao and I looked at each other, thinking, *Where the hell did this come from?*

Diep was usually a very quiet, composed, and reserved person. But he was so powerful just now, his words succinct and concise. He spoke from his heart, from his soul. It was as though he were possessed. Thao and I nodded to each other in appreciation and knew we would be saved since we were not that good. But still we were required, as a team, to speak individually on the topic, alternately with the other team.

CHAPTER 12

A Love Triangle

D ad always wanted his children to be very well-rounded in education, music, the arts, and life in general. I was not particularly gifted in music, but as with all children of the era, I tried to please my parents by taking private music lessons. Diep, my best friend, however, was extremely talented when it came to music. We enrolled in the same private music class with an older couple who would become our second parents outside of home. They were experts in many traditional Vietnamese instruments, one of which was the mandolin, the instrument we would become very familiar with.

We instantly connected emotionally with our teachers, and they treated us as if we were their own sons. Their daughter, Lan, was the only child and extremely gifted in music, as you have probably guessed. We were eleven at the time and still didn't quite get the boy-girl thing, and we were very awkward in front of her. She knew this and turned it to her advantage.

We came to our music lessons twice a week, and we looked forward to them every week. It was something different for us, getting away from the daily school routine. Diep really excelled, and soon, he would jump ahead of me, learning more advanced lessons. I struggled quite a bit, leading my teachers to say, "What Hoan lacks in talent, he certainly makes up for in effort!" That's a nice way to say I have no talent! But I didn't care! I would grow attached to their family. Diep, Lan, and I became great friends.

Over time, I felt something totally foreign to me. My fondness for Lan grew over the weeks and months we spent studying music, although she could easily be my teacher! While my feelings grew stronger, it was a very well-kept secret. I wondered if Lan noticed it at all. She probably did but didn't want to make me feel uncomfortable. I felt happier each time I came to her house for our music lessons. The three of us would play in a trio with different concertos, obviously playing down to my level of talent! These were some of the best times of my life.

What I did not realize was that Lan had feelings for Diep, and vice versa. It was also a very well-kept secret, at least from me. I was totally clueless! What an idiot! One day, on our normal break from our music lessons, I took a casual stroll to the garden, and there I felt a sense of betrayal and sadness. Diep and Lan were holding hands in the garden, talking at close range as if they were lovers! Well, of course they were! They quickly moved away from each other after noticing me walking up from behind them. That was one of the most awkward moments of my entire life—well, a short life to that point anyway. I turned and walked away quickly, embarrassed! Diep ran after me and pulled my arm from behind.

"Wait! I am sorry!" he spoke anxiously.

"For what!" I played dumb.

"I know how you feel about Lan but…" He stopped midsentence.

"It's not your fault. I guess we can't force these things!" It was a very wise thought coming from someone who was embarrassed and probably dumbstruck.

"Are you okay? I feel bad about it." Diep comforted me.

"I am good. I have to go home early today. We can catch up tomorrow. Can you tell Lan I say goodbye?" I told Diep, then walked slowly to my bike and headed home!

The bike ride was much longer and tougher than usual. Of course, my first *crush* had to be with someone who didn't even have the same feelings about me. I instantly grew up a lot that day. Maybe this was the time I grew out of being a little boy into a young man. I remember how this feeling called love, or maybe infatuation, clouded my thoughts and rendered me unable to think straight or do anything right. I needed time to recover.

It's Saturday morning, and the doorbell rang! I lazily dragged myself to the door. It was Diep, with his wide, bright smile, trying to cheer me up.

"Morning, sunshine! How're you feeling today?" he said cheerfully

I rolled my eyes and nodded reluctantly, walking back into the house, Diep following behind me.

"Listen, why don't we go down to the square today and hang out" he tried to strike up a conversation

"What the hell are you doing here so early on a Saturday anyway!" I sounded irritated.

"Well, we're best friends, and we hang out!" Diep always tried to play the "best friend" card with me

I said nothing, walking toward the kitchen. Diep hopped in front of me, still with a wide smile.

"Oh, com'on. It's a beautiful day. I know you want to go!" He had always been persistent.

"Get out of my way!" I sounded a little more aggressive than I would have liked.

"Listen. I know you're mad, hurt, and all that. But we didn't mean to hurt you. You know that, right?" He tried to diffuse the tension.

I stayed silent, letting my eyes do the talking. But deep down, I knew he was right. I just wanted to play with him a little longer, making him feel unnecessary guilt.

"You know we didn't mean to hurt you, right?" he said again in a very soft tone

"I know! It's something I have to work through. I am really happy for you guys! Really!" I finally spoke up. Diep's eyes shined, and his smile widened. He put his arm around my shoulder, and I felt a sense of relief and comfort. We stood there for a little while, in silence!

"Okay. Let me go change, and we head down to the square" I broke the silence and ran to my bedroom to change! Along the way,

I thought, *I finally grew up. I really grew up!* A sense of pride and fear came over me as I wondered if things would start changing between me and my friends as we started to grow out of our childhood. Well, I forgot to tell you all I tend to overthink a lot, with everything! I smiled as I put on my short and T-shirt, ready for a fun day in the square! Life was good. Life was very good.

CHAPTER 13

Time to Say Goodbye!

April 30, 1975, a very dark day in our history, marked the end of life as I knew it. The sirens glared, spreading the deafening sound across the capital of Saigon. People were running and screaming across the streets in total chaos in the dead of night. Dad calmly gathered all of us in the living room.

"It's time to go. It's time to say goodbye!" Dad remained calm, his voice steady and firm, but I could feel the sorrow and worries in his eyes. Mom, with her steely determination as always, looked across all of us, nodding.

"Do we really have to go, Daddy?" Mom looked at Dad. She called him Daddy with all her affection for him.

"Afraid so, Mommy!" Dad answered, his eyes fixed on Mom. He called her Mommy, as in the "mother of our children."

"But I don't want you to stay here by yourself!" Mom said, squeezing his hands tightly.

"Don't worry, Mom. I am here too." My oldest brother, Huynh, reached for Mom's shoulder.

"But..." Mom hesitated.

"We are running out of time. You got to go. Without you, what are the kids going to do?" Dad, for the first time, told Mom with desperation in his voice.

Mom, who had always been the strength of this family, seemed broken, her face saddened by years of weathering the destruction of war and keeping her children safe. She lowered her face, her eyes gazing at the living room floor. This was a goodbye unlike any other goodbyes. This is *the goodbye*, with very little hope to ever reunite ourselves as a family. Dad looked at me, for reasons I couldn't understand, as if thrusting upon me the responsibility of a caretaker even though I was only a boy. My sisters cried, emotional, knowing they would no longer be able to see Dad, our oldest brother, their teachers, and friends ever again. They stayed silent the entire time; crying was the only constant.

Uncle Van, Dad's assistant and chauffer, was by our side, awaiting Dad's order. Dad waved him over, whispering to him, "Be careful, son! Make sure they get situated before you leave." Dad told Uncle Van, calling him son and treating him like one of his children

"Yes, sir! Got it," Uncle Van said softly. He had always been a part of our family. Mom treated him like her own son as well, even though he had a family of his own. Whenever he did something not to her liking, Mom would discipline him just as she would any of us, and he absolutely loved it. He, too, called my parents Daddy and Mommy! Dad trusted him unconditionally, and he had never let Dad down. A very honest, simple, and unassuming man, always looking out for others, Mr. Van was absolutely an example of a model human being. I always admired him but gave him a lot of trouble at the same time. But he never complained, always smiling and looking after me, which was much more than a full-time job. "You are my favorite!" he always said to me, even though he had quite a time trying to keep me in line as Dad had wished. I would not hesitate to take the blame once in a while when things didn't quite go the way it should.

His voice shaken, Uncle Van came closer to me, putting his hands on my shoulder. "I guess this is goodbye!" he said softly, unable to completely hide the tears in his eyes, as I nodded.

"Come now! Go! There's no more time," Dad said, trying to scream over the loud sirens.

Each of us barely had a couple of pair of clothing for the trip to the unknown. Mom managed to stash ten US dollars for emergencies. That was all we would be able to manage. I finally felt the impending doom in front of us. How could anyone pick up and go, leaving behind years of memories, of friendships, of families, of love, of broken hearts, of shattered dreams, of unwavering hopes, of unfulfilled wishes? This was our life, this was our country, this was our soul. Despite heartaches and broken dreams, this was where we belonged. I struggled deeply to comprehend what was happening, though trying to not to let my dad and my family know what was in my heart at the time. I struggled, thinking about my friends, especially Diep, my best friend. We never had the chance to properly say goodbye. My teachers, who always tried their best to teach me, not only of the different academic subjects but, more importantly, to be a humble and good person. They were my parents at school. I struggled to come to terms with my own ideals, of who I would be and what I would do when I grew up.

This is not fair, I thought.

A sense of guilt and selfishness invaded my thoughts. I was the lucky one—we were the lucky ones—but don't say that to Mom. She would rather stay with Dad, if not for us kids. I was naive to think everything would be the way it had always been! We would struggle, but we always managed to make it through, one day at a time. But we were running out of "one day at a time." We were running out of "managing the struggles." We were running out of "playtime at the schoolyard." We were *running out of time*. This was the end. My friends and I dreaded this day would come but did not realize it would come so quickly and without the chance for a proper goodbye. I felt a sense of immense loss and sadness. My friends, my relatives, and I never had a chance to really say goodbye, and the same went for all my siblings and their friends. We knew it would be a long, long time before we would have a chance to see them again, if ever.

Dad rushed Mom and all of us on to his official military jeep, with Uncle Van driving. Dad gave Mom the *last kiss*. It was rare for us to see them showing any emotions, but this was not just *any old time*. This was *the end*! I remember Dad standing there, motionless, with a blank but sad expression on his face. We were everything to him, and he was everything to us.

Thinking back, I was never quite able to comprehend what was going on at the time or what I was actually feeling. I was just numb emotionally. I knew it was very bad, but I didn't really appreciate the veracity of the situation until much, much later. But again, I was only fourteen at the time. How much of the world would I be able to comprehend? I suddenly realized how insignificant I was, not only to the world but to everyone around me. I realized I had been a burden all these years, making absolutely no contribution worth mentioning, except my menacing shenanigans and mischief. But strangely, I didn't cry. I had always been unable to shed a tear, at least the traditional physical tear, regardless of how emotionally devastating the situation was. My heart, however, was a totally different thing altogether. If I could hold my heart in my hand, it would be a shattered beat of uncontrolled grief and a total mess. I always felt, right or wrong, that emotions should be something so private that no one except me should be entitled to their full weight. I had always been a carefree, happy-go-lucky kid in the eyes of others. Thinking back, Dad was the only one who knew I was not the person I appeared to be. I closed my eyes briefly, trying to push all my emotions inward, letting out the deepest sigh of my life. This was the end; I finally came to terms with this inevitable reality.

Mom and Uncle Van hurried us into the jeep. I turned and took one last look at my life, my childhood, my being, my heart, my soul, the home where I grew up. I saw Dad standing there, motionless, tall and thin. Little did I know that would be the very last time I had the chance to look at Dad, always strong, always confident, always tough, always caring, always loving, always teaching (me mostly!), always protecting, always nurturing, always sacrificing, always, always, always! Tears rushed through my heart like a tidal wave. This was the end!

As the jeep rolled down the main street on its way to Tan Son Nhat airfield, Vietnam International Airport, I could see people desperately running in the streets—mothers screaming, children crying in utter chaos. The deafening sound of sirens still rang through. The war was finally over, and we lost. Freedom lost! Innocence lost! Friendships lost! Family lost! Mr. Van carefully maneuvered the jeep through a sea of people running disorderly throughout the streets. The flares of artillery rang out from a distance. The loud engine noise of the tanks and warplanes of the South Vietnamese government desperately mounted the last offensive to stave off the enemies.

I often wondered about the irony, *Where did we go wrong? Why did we find ourselves here?*

It was just a philosophical difference in life and freedom that we could not overcome, even as people of the same race and country. And we paid for it ultimately, with innocent lives, sweat, and blood. As a young boy, I did not totally comprehend the magnitude of the war, the political struggles of powerful countries. But I knew Vietnam would never be the same! I would never be the same! My family and friends would never be the same! History was written that day, and I was one of the witnesses to that history, something I would not rather be.

Where do we go from here? I thought to myself on the way to the airfield. *What would happen to Dad? What would happen to our relatives, our friends, our teachers, our people, and our children across the humbled land of Vietnam?*

I was utterly useless, powerless to cope with the situation, much less do something about it. I finally realized why Dad had spent so much time telling me at a very young age how to grow up to be a responsible young man. He had his reasons, and I absolutely did not appreciate it until now, until the end!

This airlift rescue was an effort by the United States government to evacuate as many people as they could, starting with families of the military, along with American Embassy personnel, journalists, intelligence personnel, and their families! Dad told me we would be one of the lucky families to be evacuated. I remember telling him, "I'd rather be unlucky and stay with you, our family, and friends!" And for the first time, he did not think I was out of line. Maybe, secretly deep down, he wanted that as well. But he knew it got to be this way.

I look out of the jeep, at the airfield crowded with people. The airfield was lit with bright yellow lights shining on the runway. Multiple large C-130 air cargo planes were sitting on the active runway, ready to be loaded with people, potential refugees. The military soldiers and police were yelling orders to make sure people got on board. I took one last look at my beloved country. This was goodbye! This was goodbye!

The military personnel and police were extremely efficient, as they probably had to do this many times before! The back hatches of the cargo planes were all opened, revealing the massive inner bellies of the planes; one could hold up over one hundred people at a time. No one told us where we were going—not even Dad, since he probably did not know—just anywhere away from the present danger. Wave after wave of people, crying, were being loaded onto the cargo planes as orderly as could be. I looked over at Mom, profound loss and sadness written on her face. A woman in her forties should not have to be away from her husband without a chance to ever be reunited. I would never be able to understand and comprehend her loss, her emotions. That night, I grew up quickly, promising not to be the troublemaker I had always been, turning over a new leaf. I thought of my friends, of no longer having the chance to do the crazy, stupid things we pulled off over the years—no more arguments; no more smart-ass, sarcastic remarks; no more sharing a bowl of noodles; no more buying lottery tickets from the street peddlers; no more anything.

Finally, it was our turn to get on the cargo plane. We all helped Mom onto the ramp leading to the belly of the cargo plane, along with the military police. I felt as though I was walking into a prison cell, forever changing our lives, to a destination unknown. This was the end! We were all sitting on the floor of the cargo plane, hands clutching the insignificant belongings we managed to bring along with us. In a matter of a few hours, we would no longer be on our soil, the land we called home, the land we grew up in, and the land on which we built our futures. Several more families climbed into the belly of our cargo plane, filling it up quickly, everyone clinging to their own families.

The back hatch of the plane rose slowly, shutting us in this prison cell, blocking us from the outside world for the time being. I was too tired to be able to think. Maybe this was for the better. The exhaustion allowed me a brief time to forget! The cargo plane roared loudly as the two engines on each side ignited, signaling us it was time to go. It was time to say goodbye. It was time to leave behind everything we knew. It was time to finally feel the full impact of the war. It was time to appreciate and hang on to every single memory we could, as time was getting ready to erase our present lives and prepare for the new ones ahead of us. I was tired. I got to sleep. It was the dead of night. It was the final goodbye. When I woke up, it would be a new day, in a new, strange place, away from all I had ever known. I was exhausted. It was the final goodbye! I fell into a difficult sleep, with my head in between my knees.

It would be okay, I told myself. *A new day and new world awaits me.*

CHAPTER 14

Here's to a New Adventure!

The cargo plane's engines purred in unison. The vibrations underneath my seat on the plane floor were part therapeutic, part numbing, I fell deep into a much-needed sleep…

*****

I was on my way to the music academy. It was one of those things my dad insisted would round me out as a person. I was not what people would call a musically inclined person. I didn't have the talent or the patience for it. I admired my classmates, who seemed to gravitate to the mystery I called music. What I lacked in talent, I guess I made up for with hard work. It seemed as though I had to rely on hard work to make up for many of my deficiencies. At least, that was what all my teachers told me. It didn't hurt my feelings since I knew I really didn't have any real talents. As much as I told my dad I didn't like music, I had to admit sometimes it was a great escape from the daily ugliness of war, the senseless deaths, and the torture of destruction. It was one of those things that brought some normalcy to my life, even though it seemed like torture at times. I knew my dad tried to provide me with a path to escape from the ravages of war, and I loved him for that. Even though I deliberately tried to fight back, deep down I really respected and appreciated him trying to make me a better person. Obviously, I wouldn't have become who I was without his vision and guidance.

The Academy, as it was simply called, was full of talented children and musicians, some as young as five years old. I felt grossly inferior and incompetent compared to other, much more gifted children. They were musical geniuses. It seemed as though they could play music before they could speak or read. I always found that so amazing. They played away tirelessly as I continued to struggle through even the simplest classical pieces. Like my teacher said, what I lacked in talent I made up for with hard work. That was what I did to survive the "arts." I worked hard on every concerto we had to play. For the next few years, I barely passed the necessary exams to get through to the next level. The other children got better every year, while I struggled to maintain my level of musical mediocrity. One positive note, though: I made a lot of friends while I was there, mostly because they felt sorry for me. It seemed like I was the only kid who didn't belong there. But somehow, I managed!

*****

The plane shook violently as it encountered strong turbulence. I snapped back to reality, stealing a look around me. Everyone looked exhausted and sad. Mom sat still, back to the side of the plane, eyes looking out at nothing in particular! It must be devastating for her, thinking of her husband, my dad. They had never been apart, ever, until now. She was only one of the women who had to bear the burden of caring for her family from now on, not knowing exactly where she would end up and without the person who had been there with her all this time. I felt a tinge of guilt, knowing there was nothing I could do to improve the situation. I decided to spare Mom the triviality of asking her how she was doing, how she felt, and all that nonsense—maybe later but definitely not now. The cargo plane recovered its balance after a few minutes of struggling with Mother Nature. There were three military police officers in the belly of the plane with us, looking out for our safety. I looked at them in uniform, my mind racing back to the image of my dad coming home from a long day, also in his uniform. It was a very hard life. While Dad never mentioned it to any of us children, I was sure he and Mom talked about it often. The immense pressure of guarding freedom and protecting innocent lives weighed heavily on Dad, but he kept at it day after day while hiding it from all of us. I felt guilty and useless again, but I was too exhausted to care. I fell back into my sleep—the only way I knew how to get away from the current predicament and to a place far away—my happy place!

*****

It was the New Year's Festival in Vietnam. I was full of anticipation and excitement. I woke up early that day and had it all planned out. I put on my newest outfit, a bright-red shirt (for luck) and black shorts. I looked around the house and saw that my mom and sisters had decorated it with colorful ornaments and fireworks. I couldn't help but smile at the festive mood, not just in my house but in the whole neighborhood. We had a whole week off from school to celebrate, for New Year's is the biggest and most important holiday in Vietnam. I climbed on my bicycle and started pedaling toward my best friend's house. I pedaled very fast, afraid I would be losing valuable time from the day. I must have smiled all the way to his house from the funny looks people gave me along the streets. But that was the one day I didn't mind what people thought. He dressed up as well, in a bright-yellow shirt and blue shorts. We had planned to set off some fireworks of our own. I had a pocket full of small pieces of fireworks taken from my dad's private stash. This was a tradition for me and Diep, my best friend. He got on his bike the minute he saw me. We began pedaling toward the cemetery behind the neighborhood. We felt the people who were laid to rest deserved to hear the festive sounds of New Year's as well, just like the living. With pride filling our hearts, we set off to the cemetery, fireworks in our shorts' pockets. Life was simple and good at that moment. We didn't talk much, but we knew what the other was thinking.

The streets were very festive. Young boys and girls dressed in their brightest and newest outfits, ready to bring in the New Year. The broad smiles masked the sadness and anxiety of a people at war. It was the year of the monkey, not that it mattered. Diep and I observed the people walking, biking, running, and talking. It was an amazing sight. The streets were jam-packed. So many children blocking the streets in their outfits, laughing, made me appreciate my life. The vendors tried harder than most days to sell all their goods before retiring for the New Year. This was the time to look for bargains, not that I had any money to buy anything. We lived a very modest, average life, but it was a very happy and spiritual life. Diep and I continued to bike carefully through the crowd, looking at things, wishing we had money to buy. But we knew we wouldn't be able to do that until after the New Year. It was a tradition during New Year's that children received red envelopes filled with money (*Li` Xi`* is the Vietnamese term for it) from their elders. The thoughts of receiving those red envelopes, having no school for a week, eating as much as we want, and doing no chores got all the children excited about New Year's.

I told Diep, "We can come back and buy those things we want once we get our red envelopes!"

Diep replied, "Yeah, I know! It'll be fun!"

*****

The captain's voice came over the speakers, "We are touching down in roughly thirty minutes. Please prepare the plane and get ready to land."

One of the military police officers, an American who spoke Vietnamese fluently, translated the captain's message as he spoke to the future refugees, getting them ready for landing.

"Please make sure you put your head between your knees and hold still when I give you the signal. It's important to prevent any unpredicted movements of the plane due to turbulence." He looked around, seeing heads nodding, indicating everyone understood what to do.

My mind was drifting again with only a short time left on the flight. I recalled that it was a cloudy day when we left earlier, befitting the mood of the day when everything ended.

*****

It was a cloudy, dark Saturday, the summer of 1968. I drifted to a familiar place. It was one of those ordinary days, but somehow I could feel something was different. I was at my usual Sunday get-to-gether with my friends. We rode our bikes around the busy market streets in our neighborhood. We talked about school, people, friends, family, etc. I had been bothered by a strange feeling that day, and Diep, my best friend, could tell. There were five of us, the Fun Pack, as I called us. I was preoccupied that day and didn't exactly know why. But I tried my best to have fun that day. We barely had enough money to buy each of us one bowl of noodle (*Pho* in Vietnamese) at our usual corner noodle shop. Afterward, we went to the nearby deserted pond and threw little rocks in the water to create the illusion of waves. None of us talked a lot that day. It was probably my fault, but I didn't seem to pay any attention. Just right after noon, we decided to call it a day and rode our separate ways. Diep was trying to stay close to me after the others left. We didn't live that far away from each other, so he decided to ride home with me. He started the minute we were alone.

"Is something wrong?" he said.

"Not really. It's just something I am feeling right now, and I don't quite know what it is. So I can't tell you. You know that I will tell you if I know, right?" I said absentmindedly.

"I know, I know!" he said.

"Well! I have to go. I'll see you tomorrow, okay?" I said quietly.

"Sure. If you need anything, let me know, okay?" he said, his voice worried.

We rode silently home the rest of the way. It was almost one o'clock in the afternoon when I finally made it home. Everyone was home except my oldest and second oldest brothers. They were rarely home at that time anyway. They always seemed to have things to do, people to see. I went to my room, and immediately, my mom was curious. She followed me shortly afterward.

"Are you okay, honey?" she asked with tenderness in her voice.

"I'm fine, Mom, just tired!" I answered quietly.

"If you need anything, call me!" she said as she left the room…

*****

"We are landing in ten minutes!" the captain's voice came over the speakers again as the military police officers stood and went around the belly of the plane, checking in to make sure every passenger was locked in, assuming the proper position for landing. When everything was done, they went back and settled into their seats, hiding their emotions very well.

I held Mom's hands, squeezing them tightly to reassure her it that would be okay. She nodded knowingly; sadness remained in her eyes. She seemed to have aged several years since this journey began. For the first time, I began to comprehend the cruel reality of no longer being on home soil. We had reached the point of no return. For better or worse, we had decided to escape our falling country, falling democracy, and falling freedom. I felt how unfair life was at that moment. Families taken away from families, children torn away from parents, and wives from husband were the unacceptable consequences of war!

I began to be exposed to what the real world could be like. While I knew cruelty and injustice existed in this world, there was also kindness and generosity that would conquer all. I remembered my father's words once more: "This is the reason why you should always thrive to become a decent man, a decent human being!"

*****

We were on our way to our usual hangout spot, Pho Tau Bay (a popular noodle shop in Saigon), on a bright, beautiful Sunday. Most Sundays in Vietnam during the sunny season were fairly hot and humid. I was daydreaming on the back of my dad's motorcycle, like I always did on every outing with him on Sundays, about things that might not matter much to anyone else—school, friends, breaks, playgrounds, etc.

My dad started in on his conversation, "You know, son, it's never too early to learn about the reality of life and how you can make a difference in this world. Take, for example, the things around you now. I know the war seems hopeless, and the devastation is beyond our imagination. But everyone can do his or her own part to help. Ask yourself one question, son: 'What can I do to contribute to a better tomorrow?'"

I remember thinking to myself, *Dad, I'm only twelve! That's a very difficult question for a twelve-year-old!* Instead, I answered, "I can and should always try to better myself."

He was focusing on the road but managed to say, "Well, that's a good start. What else can you do to offer society?"

I forced myself to think harder, anticipating that my dad was trying to teach me a very valuable life lesson.

"Well, Dad, I can do the best I can at all times at everything I do. Does that count?" I replied.

"Of course it does, son. It always does. I know you feel that you're too young to think about these things. But our country is not like any other, son. We are living in a different time. Things don't stay the same for very long. We have to make sure we can change quickly to adapt to change." My dad's voice was full of passion and commitment. "Being a decent and kind human being and becoming a man of principles will be difficult because you're being challenged constantly. Our country is desperately poor. People are always tempted to do something against moral principles and integrity. Do you understand, son?"

"Kinda, Dad!" I replied

"Living within moral principles in a society like ours will require a lot of discipline. You must remember that material possessions mean nothing if you have to trade your soul for them," he continued in a very serious way.

"I'll try, Dad! I know that when the time comes, I'll always do the best I can. That's all I can promise you."

"That's more than I can ask for, son, that you'll always try to do your best to live your life the way you never have to regret. Live every day as if it will be your last. You need to remember to live with passion, love for family, love for country, a sense of community, and human kindness. If you can do that, you can never go wrong." Even though I couldn't see his eyes, I could tell he was beaming with pride and hope.

"I promise I will always try to do that, Dad...always!" I told him quietly.

"Now, after all that, I bet you're ready to eat. You're starving, aren't you?" he said with a chuckle in his voice.

"Yes, Dad! Very!" I told him excitedly.

His Vespa came to a stop, and we walked together quietly with his right hand on my shoulder. He didn't have to say anything else. I began to understand what my dad was saying. I never imagined his teaching would someday guide me through the path ahead. These teachings and these words would later give me the balance and compass to build a strong new life. But for now, there was a little matter of survival to worry about, and I would need all the strength I could muster to see it through—for me, for Mom, for my family, but mostly for my own pride and sanity.

*****

Our cargo plane finally landed safely. The back hatch slowly opened, and there was a heavy thump as the landing ramp automatically slid out from the bottom of the plane. The three military officers quickly jumped off the plane and began giving orders in Vietnamese.

"Please get up slowly. You have been sitting for a long time, roughly three hours to be exact. Make sure you stand up slowly until you can regain your balance. For the elderly people, please help them up and make sure they are okay before you deplane," the youngest of the officers spoke with compassion in his voice. "Once you make it down, please stand to the side of the ramp, and we will take a count to make sure everyone is accounted for. Please let us know if you don't feel well, and we will make sure you will be provided medical assistance while we are here! Once we had a chance to count and check you off the list, we will let you know what will happen next. Please ask if you have any questions!"

I sat down on the ground once I got off the plane, head between my knees, occasionally glancing at my mom. I barely paid attention to a single word the military officer said, my mind occupied with thoughts far away from this place. Mom looked exhausted and emotionally drained. I remember how strong she was, taking care of our family, working with a small book stand to help support our family, along with Dad.

*****

She sat at the back, in a little space at the corner of one of the busiest streets in downtown Saigon. We needed extra money, and she was one of those people who would feel useless if she sat at home. My mom was always a fighter. She was the glue that kept everything running smoothly in our family. I admired her strength and resolve. She always seemed to have an idea of what she wanted to do and how she wanted to do it. She loved her family, although at times I challenged that notion because I always got into trouble and tried to get away with it. Looking back, I felt fortunate.

She began laying out the books in a specific order, day after day. It was three o'clock in the afternoon, and I went to the corner store after school. I always came down to help. My job was to look for used books from people who put them up for sale, and she sold them back to people who wanted to buy them. I fitted the role perfectly, taking advantage of my innocent look at ten and getting a lot of books *cheap*! I also had the knack for making people interested in the books we had to sell. My mom usually sat back and collected the money. I felt useful helping her out.

My mom was a determined woman. She always managed to have everything organized at home. She didn't show much emotion most of the time, but her love for my dad and the children was unquestioned. She was a committed wife and mother. In a society where women were viewed as inferior to men, she illuminated strength and determination throughout her partnership with my dad. They gave us children a sense that even though war was raging on, there was still stability in our everyday lives.

I always thought it was amazing that even though a lot of women in Vietnam took care of the entire household, their rights were limited. I remember running into Vietnamese women who started selling early in the morning whatever goods they could to support their families but yet had no say in how the families were being run. It was also evident that the men in these families (a lot of them in my own neighborhood) totally lacked a sense of responsibility and accountability. Yet they were able to scream at their wives and children to show they were in total control. As I observed these men, I couldn't help but admire my dad. He was a pioneer in his own right. He was a person of few words yet very firm in the way he handled discipline in our home. He respected my mom and considered her an equal partner. This was rare at that time and could be construed as a weakness in our society. But my dad didn't care what others thought, for he knew our family was built on respect and love. I was too young to really notice how society treated these women in general. I considered myself very fortunate. My childhood was somewhat uneventful, except for my own stubbornness, which tended to get me into trouble from time to time (unintentionally, of course!).

*****

"It's time to get all of you situated. We are in Clark Air Base in the Philippines. You will remain here for several months while we process your refugee status. We will let you know when we get closer to where you would go and how you will get there! But for now, I will suggest for everyone to settle in and be as comfortable as you can. We will be here for a while!" The young officer spoke again with a bullhorn, dragging me away from my brief daydream.

I saw a row of buses lined up at the side of the Clark Air Base runway, each visibly numbered. I walked over to Mom to check on her. My siblings were also visibly exhausted, physically and emotionally. They began loading us on different buses, doing so by family. I thought of my friends and wondered what they were doing. I miss them terribly! I looked up at the night sky, full of stars, full of hope, and full of love. Somewhere out there, far away, my childhood somehow survived and thrived through all the adversities, due in no small part to the love and care of my friends.

*****

My friends and I played hooky for the day. It was my master plan. It always seemed to be my master plan when it came to breaking the rules. We met early this morning with our backpacks full of stuff. Each of us was holding our favorite fishing rod. It wasn't much of a rod, really, just a long piece of string on a sturdy stick, courtesy of a big tree in my backyard. We brought along some bread, noodles, and water. The pond was unusually quiet today. The peaceful breeze brought some much-needed relief from the intense heat all week. We picked our usual spots under a big tree, not only for the shade but also because we had staked our claim there by carving our names into it. It was one of those childhood rituals we did. "Friends Forever!" it said. Times were tough as the war got more intense. This was our escape from the harsh reality of it all. We were tired of dealing with the grief of losing loved ones. It affected us all. We were more than friends. We were an extended family. All of our parents know all of us. We were all their children.

I looked at Diep, my best friend. He seemed happy and shot a bright smile back at me. Nhat, his brother, was the sensible person in our group. Thao, our classmate, was the self-absorbed one. He was a great friend and person. We teased him often for the fact that he seemed to pay the most attention to himself. Huong was the most caring person in our group. She made sure we were prepared for any adventures we cooked up. She was a genuinely humble and loving person. Lan was the shy one of the group. She never said much when we hung out together, but we knew she belonged. We could all tell her heart and mind were with us at all times. She had a quiet way of looking at people, and her smile could melt any troubles away. She had a gift!

We laid our gear down by the trunk of our favorite tree and began unpacking our stuff. The sky was a perfect blue, and we hoped the fish would be biting. We needed to make hot and sour fish soup. I promised my mom I would catch at least a big fish to feed the whole family. I looked around and smiled secretly to myself. I was the luckiest person in the whole world.

*****

"Are you okay, son?" Mom's voice brought me back.

"I am good, Mom. I worry about you. You good?" I asked.

"Yes, good. We will have time to deal with everything once we settle in," Mom said, always very practical and never letting her emotions show. She was the symbol of strength, always.

We made our way up to bus number 5, with each bus holding around sixty people. Our family took two rows on each side, each with two seats. I settled in by the window, staring out at the open field, wondering what life would be like. The bus gently left the airfield, pulling the stars in the sky along with it. I leaned against the chilling window, falling into another undeserved sleep.

*****

Christmas lights were lit brightly everywhere. I dressed excitedly and quickly, trying not to miss any minute of the magical spirit of the holiday season. It was my favorite time of the year. Although not Catholic, I still found the holiday season fascinating. People were happier. It was not so much a religious holiday as it was a time for family and friends to celebrate love and togetherness. I raced out to the backyard and climbed on my bike.

"Be careful!" I heard Mom's gentle voice as she smiled at me.

"Thanks, Mom! I will."

I pedaled briskly as the wind brushed against my face. It felt really good.

Freedom! I thought.

I smiled at the thought of meeting up with my friends at the cathedral. Something about the holiday season, being a teenager, and meeting up with friends stirred great emotions in me. I felt blessed to have a wonderful family and great friends. Life was simple, despite the intense and devastating war. Every newscast on the radio updated the casualties and damages. Schools, rice fields, churches, and temples were destroyed through the intense bombing campaigns from both sides, North and South. Maybe I was used to putting things in the back of my mind. If you lived here long enough, you would develop a numbness that enabled you to block out all the bad stuff. War was a part of everyday life. We focused on family, friends, and our future, just like any other child across the world, despite the war.

A burst of cold air hit my face and brought me back to the joy and excitement I had anticipated. I approached the crowded cathedral. Motorbikes and bicycles jammed the front gate. I felt the adrenaline surge inside me as I broke out with goose bumps. I saw Diep first with his signature "loose" hair and his sharp, big eyes. He waved in my direction as I slowly pedaled through the crowd. The voices were deafening. People were talking and laughing, making animated gestures with their hands in all directions. There were too many people in such a very small space, just the way things had always been in Vietnam.

I finally made it to Diep and saw Nhat, his brother; Lan; Thao; and Huong. They dressed in their new clothes for the new holiday season. We just looked at each other without saying a word. And then, we all smiled simultaneously. Yes, we were the best of friends. We locked up our bikes and started squeezing through the crowd on our way inside the cathedral courtyard. It was elegant and full of lights tonight. Even though we were not Catholics, we always enjoyed and appreciated the elaborate decorations at Christmastime.

We made our way to the gigantic manger, built from huge, solid rocks. Strands of thick white rope, yarn, and cotton were stretched over the anterior rocks of the manger to give the feel of real snow. Inside the manger, the soft and gentle yellow light seemed to emit heat and warmth. All the statues lay on a soft bed of hay. We stood in silence for a long time, just staring at the enormous manger. I stole a peek at my friends, feeling ecstatic. In a country ravaged by war, these people represented what goodness is all about. They were all unique in their own ways, always reaching out to others. "Only a kind heart can overcome tragedies!" my mom always reminded us. The people who stood next to me definitely overcame their own tragedies and reached out to ease others', especially during this time of year. I turned back to the manger. The lights somehow grew softer. I was at peace and happy.

We walked through the entire courtyard, a constant cool breeze brushing through the soft air.

"So how did you do on your finals?" Huong spoke up to the entire group.

"I did okay on the math test. I don't like literature. I think it's a waste of time!" Nhat, the more practical person in the group, replied.

"That's because you don't appreciate the deep meaning of things around you." Lan sounded irritated with him but in a good way. Lan was a die-hard romantic. She was the best in our group when it came to poetry and literature.

"Oh, no! I appreciate many deep meanings of things around me, like you, Lan, Huong," Nhat shot back with his signature mischievous grin, clearly trying to further irritate Lan.

"See what I mean. You make a joke about it," Lan spoke as she turned her back to him. I couldn't help but smile at the exchange.

"Maybe Nhat thinks he can make numbers behave like words. Who knows? There are many deeper, hidden meanings to numbers. And Nhat can make those numbers come to life and impress all of you," I said half jokingly.

"That's exactly what I'm trying to say." Nhat smiled broadly as he tapped on Lan's shoulder. She gave him a cold stare, sending chills down my spine.

"So what about you, Huong?" I asked.

"Oh! I did okay. Nothing spectacular. I think I passed all the exams," Huong replied unenthusiastically. Huong was more focused on the social aspects of school. She usually chaired all the social events at school. "Social Queen," we called her. She was quite flattered by the title.

"I think I aced most of my exams," Thao finally spoke up. True to form, his full-of-himself persona came through.

"That goes without saying!" I fueled his ego even further as he broke into a big laugh. "Diep, what about you?" I continued.

"I did well on most of my exams, I think. I had a little trouble with my math exam, though." Diep was our art guru. He loved theater, arts, music, and anything abstract. He served as our class's head of entertainment, managing everything from the school yearbook to school plays. He definitely had the talent for them.

I, on the other hand, was the most average of all of my friends. The only talent I seemed to have was bringing all of my friends together.

CHAPTER 15

A New Life

The bus stopped in front of the old, abandoned military barracks, with cots for beds. Each family was taken to its assigned barracks and designated rooms. I was too exhausted to think, walking like a zombie to the orders of the military officers. Mom and the rest of our family settled into barrack number 9. They all looked the same except for the number identifying them. We threw our minimal belongings on the floor as soon as we made it to our room. I climbed on the cot in the corner of the room, curling up and falling into a very deep sleep, too tired to even manage a dream. I slept as if I hadn't slept in years.

The beautiful sunlight was shining through the big windows on the barrack, pulling me up on my cot, ready to face a new day. The military officers came around to each barrack, giving us the run-through for the day.

"Each day you can go down to the cafeteria (they called it the mess hall in military terms) for breakfast, lunch, and dinner at specific assigned times. Everyone needs to be present to get their food. Each of you will be given a card for each member of your family. If you are getting food for someone else, you cannot do it all at one time. You have to get in line each time to get one portion for each person. They will stamp each meal to make sure everyone gets to eat properly. Any questions?" the young military officer said to a quiet barracks, indicating we understood.

With my siblings being mostly women, I was the designated person getting these meals for our family. I didn't mind doing that. Being very young, active, and able, I took it on. So life went on, day after day, for three months. I got in line eight times for breakfast, eight times for lunch, and eight times for dinner to get food for my entire family. Initially, Mom did not eat much. She was not used to the food there, and I assumed she still missed Dad too much to eat. But I performed my chores dutifully, day after day. Life went on uneventfully as if nothing had happened. No one talked about the war; no one talked about the toll it took on them and their families. There was a silent understanding among the families.

It was time to move on. We were finally going to Guam Island, a United States territory, to prepare to enter the United States, awaiting sponsorship to our assigned final destination.

It really doesn't matter where we go! I thought to myself.

I struggled to find my footing again, having a routine like the one I had in Vietnam. We were living a temporary life—no home, no school, and no friends. I struggled to regain my confidence, my stability, and myself. But these were extraordinary times, and I needed to adjust. I packed what little belongings I had, getting ready to get on another flight to Guam. I checked in on Mom to make sure she was still okay. She said she felt okay, but she aged a lot more than I remembered, losing weight. I worried about the toll it all was having on her. But for now, we had to keep moving. This was the *beginning*! This was the *beginning*!

They loaded us up on another cargo plane on the way to Guam. The heat was unbearable as we landed in the middle of the afternoon and were taken to a large open field. Simple military tents, each holding four people, lined the field, with portable toilets in each section. The red dust, scattered from the ground by the heavy wind, made it very difficult to breathe. We went through the same drill, settling into our assigned tents. I began making mental notes of the unique markings around our tents. We were assigned two tents, seemingly in the middle of the field, surrounded by other tents. I picked up on the large flagpole with the US flag to the right of our tents. I smiled approvingly, remembering this flagpole as the central point of our tents, just in case I got lost.

Everyone struggled with the extreme heat, and not long after, my entire family fell ill, probably due to dehydration. Mom was my primary concern, and I asked Tuyet to make sure she was well hydrated. We had to get in line for everything, from clean water to wash our faces and brush our teeth daily to washcloths, toilet paper, breakfasts, lunches, and dinners. Again, I, being young and healthy, assumed the responsibility of bringing all supplies and meals to our family daily. I made multiple trips and got in multiple lines every single day for each necessity, from clean water to toilet paper to each meal of the day. The heat was relentless, day and night! But I decided not to let the situation overcome me.

We would be there for one week, processing our refugee status and papers and being inspected for our health, prior to getting into the United States. It seemed much longer than a week. The multiple long lines for supplies in the extreme heat finally got to me. On the day we were to board the plane for America, I came down with a high fever and sweat. But there was no time to rest. We were heading for Fort Chaffee, Arkansas, the final landing spot, temporarily while we waited for sponsorship from America to determine where we would end up living as our new home.

Mom didn't seem too concerned, telling us, "It doesn't really matter where we go now that we are no longer in Vietnam. It will all be the same! We just have to stick to family, and everything will be okay"—classic Mom's wise advice.

I was lying on my cot when the military officers rounded us up, getting us ready to board the plane for Arkansas. I could barely move, but I gathered myself for the journey. Lucky for me, I didn't have that much belongings to worry about, just a small cloth bag with two pairs of clothing. The sun set on the far end of the sky, a hot, bright orange. It was probably always there, but I was too busy surviving to realize it until today. I stood still for a long while looking at the sunset, mesmerized.

"Okay, ladies and gentlemen. It's time to go. When I call your name, please step forward and follow this officer onto the plane! I will call you and your family at one time so you can be close to each other! Welcome to America, everyone. Fort Chaffee, Arkansas, is our next destination! We will provide food and water on this flight. It will be a very long flight, over fifteen hours. So please make sure you wear something comfortable. We have restrooms on the planes for your use! Please get ready," the young military officer said over the bullhorn in perfect Vietnamese! I couldn't help but smile in astonishment!

The military officer was not joking when he said it would be a very long flight, but at least we were on a Boeing 737 with comfortable seats and all the conveniences, unlike the C-130 cargo planes we took from Vietnam to Clark Air Base in the Philippines. I could still feel the numbness on my butt from the vibrations of the plane floor on that three-hour flight. I took the window seat, wanting to always look out the window for absolutely no apparent reason.

The plane flew high above the clouds. I looked out at the night sky, wondering what was next on this already exhausting journey.

The sky is limitless, and yet we can't find peace and freedom in our own home. This journey highlights the biggest contradiction in life. Some people would destroy and kill to take control of land and people who should never be controlled or owned! I thought.

We had to escape our own homeland to enjoy the fundamental right of every human being alive on earth: *freedom*! Freedom to think, freedom to speak, freedom to laugh, freedom to cry, freedom to walk, freedom to run—all should be the most basic fundamental rights! This journey was about the human spirit—unwavering, unapologetic, untainted, unmovable, uncontrollable, and unconquerable.

"The sky is the *limit*! The *world* is your *oyster*!" I remember the words of my history teacher, Ms. Kim. The world fascinated me, for better or for worse!

There are people who want to take over the world, even though it does not belong to them! I preferred to be *part of the world*, united among all peoples!

The sky outside the plane window cradled me into a much-needed delicious sleep.

*****

Diep and I biked our way to the television studio every Sunday for our Sunday children's show, taping *Gió Khơi* (*The Children of the Wind*). While I was not as talented as my best friend in music, I was much better at acting. Every Sunday, the show featured a variety of repertoire, always starting out with a classic tune with all the children playing ancient, historical Vietnamese instruments. I was among one of twenty children selected for the band, conducted by my private teachers, Lan's parents.

One big, popular feature of the show was the thirty-minute play, where I was a regular. Each week, we would perform a different play (fable in nature) with a lesson learned at the end. For whatever reason, I always ended up playing the character where they would say at the end, "Now, children, *don't* grow up to be like Hoan's character!"

"Why am I always playing the *bad* character, sir?" I asked my teacher one time.

"Well, son, because you're a very good actor, you made those characters come to life, and you made them *believable* to the audience!" my teacher would tell me.

"Thank you, sir!" I would say, wondering if what he said was actually a compliment.

My family was a moderate, average family. We rarely watched television, owning a small nine-inch black-and-white classic television some would call ancient. Sunday evenings, at six o'clock, my family would gather in the small, cozy living room, watching the *Children of the Wind* episode I taped the week before. I always felt embarrassed whenever they pointed to the television and said, "There's Hoan. He looks great!" How embarrassingly childish of them. Every time that happened, I would give them the "I need to go to the restroom" excuse. They never bought into it but decided to let me get away with it. How pretentiously generous of them.

*****

The plane shook violently, bringing me back to reality, as the captain's voice came through the speakers, "Folks, we got some fairly strong turbulence. I will try to find some smoother air in the next fifteen minutes, flying at a higher altitude!"

The military officer translated into English as people got nervous, clutching the armrests and each other's hands. I felt Mom's left hand clutching my right hand tightly. Sensing her anxiety, I put my left hand on top, holding her left hand between my two hands and smiling gently at her. While I was not an expert flying passenger (up until this journey, I had never been on a plane, just like everyone else on this plane), somehow I did not at all get nervous. I held Mom's hand for a long while until the plane finally settled down calmly.

Finally, the plane was getting ready to land at the Fort Smith, Arkansas, airport.

"From here, folks, it will be a five-hour bus ride to Fort Chaffee, Arkansas, where you will stay a minimum of four months until you are sponsored by a charity organization. That will determine your final destination in America. When you are there at the refugee camp in Fort Chaffee, we will do health checkups and vaccinations to make sure you are healthy to enter the US. We have medical staff at Fort Chaffee and urgent care centers to take care of you while you are there! We will serve three meals a day in the mess halls, with specific scheduled times," the young military officer explained the process to us as we got ready to land. "I will be there with you until the last one leaves the camp as your interpreter. We have an information station set up at the camp to answer any questions you have. We have submitted your names to all the big charity organizations in the United States. Whichever charities selected you and your family, that's where you will settle into your new home, your new life."

I could feel the plane descending quickly, pushing my stomach to my throat. Again Mom was squeezing my hand tightly. After a few minutes, the plane landed safely, strolling along the runway and coming to a complete stop.

"Please stay seated! I will call your names in order by family, and you can deplane. Once you get to the bottom of the stairs, please stay to the right and wait until everyone has a chance to get off the plane. Once we are done, I will take you all inside, get you processed, and rest for a couple of hours! We will then have you on buses heading to Fort Chaffee to get you checked in," the young military officer spoke to us, and I noticed that throughout this journey, he was the constant face of the assistance, speaking in perfect Vietnamese. His expression never changed! He took really good care of us in a very respectful and polite manner. I began to observe and noticed a big difference between the American and Vietnamese cultures, at least when it came to communication and manners.

Before long, we settled into several charter buses with very comfortable, big seats—much bigger for someone as small as I was. I tried to pronounce Fort Chaffee in my head, trying to at least be able to say the name of the place I would be settling in for the next several months! I began to get used to the word *refugee*. To me, it meant someone without a home, running away from oppression, or seeking freedom. I settled into my preferred window seat in the middle of the bus. I became numb to the process of moving from one place to another on this journey, punctuating the uncertainty of where our lives were heading. Would I ever find peace and stability?

You still have your whole life ahead of you, son! Dad's words came to me clearly. I wondered if this was what he had in mind when he told me that. If it was, he was more certain than I was of finding myself in this predicament. Maybe I had a long life ahead of me, yes, but a quality life was another matter. I would have to rely on my spirit, my will, my determination, my passion for the world, and my "never give up" stubbornness.

The buses started rolling out of the Fort Smith airfield in the late afternoon, traveling down nice, paved roads, the lights of which I had never seen before, long stretch after long stretch at great speed. I fell into my usual habit—leaning my head on the big bus window, staring out at rows and rows of trees passing in rhythm on the side of the long road, with only a few cars in front of us.

*****

Our group biked together down the busy Nguyen Hue Street, with trees lining the middle roundabouts and stretching the entire length of the street. This was one of our favorite things to do, especially in the evening with the light, cool breeze in our faces. The trees almost lined up perfectly, of equal height, with lovers stealing a seat underneath the big trees, sharing feelings and kisses. On either side of the streets came the loud noises of people talking, laughing as they shop, and bargaining with shop owners. Most of the time, our group did not shop. We were more into people watching, learning important human behaviors and emotions from the thousands of people crowding this main street.

*****

We were finally pulling up to an enormous area filled with white buildings, exactly alike except for the numbers on them, lining both sides of the field in perfect harmony. It looked like something straight out of a painting I used to see somewhere. All the buses pulled into huge parking lots, a different one for each section of buildings. It instantly reminded me of the unused military barracks at Clark Air Base in the Philippines but in much better shape. The building our refugee group was dropped off in front of says "Building # 11" in big, bold black print.

Everyone dragged their feet from sitting too long on the bus! My sister Tuyet and I helped Mom maneuver the steps of the building. Our rooms were on the second floor, making it a little more challenging for Mom and other elderly people. Each room had one twin bed and four bunk beds, for a total of five people. There were two full-service community bathrooms with shower stalls to be shared among the refugees, one for men and one for women. It was time to settle into our new home, at least for the next few months! Everyone was too tired to care!

Tomorrow is a new day! I will explore soon! I told myself as I settled into the top bunk bed in the room, falling asleep almost instantly, too tired to even dream!

CHAPTER 16

Starting My Own Business

The next morning, we made our way to the mess hall to get our breakfast. Mom and my siblings were not as flexible and adaptable when it came to food, the opposite of me. I didn't pay much attention to how the food tasted; my primary purpose was to fill my stomach. I assumed the "get every meal for the family" duty as if it were a born right. The mess halls here were much bigger, and more people were manning the different food stations. I typically made at least four trips every meal, holding two full plates of food at a time. For breakfast, your typical scrambled eggs, bacon, orange juice, and toast were the mainstays of the menu, day in and day out. Lunches and dinners saw a variety of dishes, although arranged by even days and odd days, so there were really only two different menus. I could certainly understand why, what with serving so many people at a time.

We still held on to our ten US dollars from the start of the trip. It had been almost seven months since we left Vietnam. I thought of Dad; Huynh, my oldest brother; my relatives; my friends; and my teachers. Dad must worry a lot, not knowing where we were since there was no way for us to communicate. My daydreams got cut short every day in exchange for the "getting in line for the daily necessities" responsibility. I didn't mind it, really. It gave me a chance to get out of the building and explore!

One day, I got an early start, walking around the refugee complex before having to get in line to get our lunches. I stumbled upon a big, beautifully manicured green field. There were people seemingly swinging long, thin sticks, trying to strike small white balls resting on a very small wooden peg, their bodies seemingly contorted and twisted. I watched in absolute astonishment. There must have been over twenty men along the path I was on, separated by a wire fence stretching the entire field. I stumbled upon a small white ball, almost falling forward. I picked up the ball, wondering. I saw a man at a washing station slipping the ball into a small, round slot, pulling the lever back and forth, and the dirty ball instantly shone as he wiped it dry with a soft cloth. An idea hatched in my troublemaking head.

What if? I thought, now deliberately looking for more small white balls that had inadvertently made their way over the fence.

To my satisfaction and calculations, there were many, many such balls along the other side of the fence of the manicured greens. I collected the balls of different brands, using my T-shirt as a bag and holding as many balls as I could. I stopped at the closest washing station, dropped the balls on the ground, washed them one by one, and dried them off using my T-shirt. They looked just as shiny as the one the gentleman I saw earlier held in his hand.

While I did not know much about the currency in the United States, but I did learn through reading about the different denominations, from a penny, a nickel, a dime, a quarter, a dollar, and so on. I decided I would corner the market for "lost small balls," not even knowing what sport they were playing. I gave my new business a "tryout." Resting on the fence along the route, I called out to a couple of men on the small, perfectly manicured green circle with a hole and a small flag sticking out of it.

"Hello. You buy!" I called out to them, holding up a couple of shiny small balls I just washed! To my surprise, they strolled toward me, towering over me.

"Wow, those are clean, son!" one of them said, smiling broadly. "Hey, Joh, how much you think we should give him?" he called out to the other man, now walking toward him.

"Maybe a quarter?" the other man said.

"That sounds fair!" The man turned toward me. "Would you take a quarter for it, son?" he said to me.

My command of the English language was still in its very early infancy, and the only word I made out of the whole sentence was quarter, which was the only thing that mattered anyway. I nodded coolly, not letting them in on my plan and excitement.

"How many?" I asked.

"Four!" the man answered, handing me a dollar bill in exchange for the cleaned, small white balls.

"Thank you, sir!" I said calmly.

Time to move on to the next customer. If this business worked, I could earn extra money to get my family a few luxury items, like soda pops and nice cookies, at the snack stations they had throughout the complex serving military personnel. But it took money, and this new business idea I cooked up just might work.

I was right! By the end of that day, I managed to make $10, the same amount of money we managed to have with us on this journey! I felt exhilarated and, for the first time, *useful*, momentarily able to forget all the devastation, destruction, and the emotional toll of war—a temporary relief from missing Dad, relatives, friends, teachers, and home.

Tomorrow will be a new day! I told myself, clutching the $10 in my shorts pocket, not yet ready to tell my family of the new, lucrative business I cooked up. *In time! In time.* I smiled—happy—and jogged home with a spring in my step. Welcome to your *new life*!

There was a knock on the door of our room one morning. I came to the door, and there was a tall, big military officer with a badge "MP" on his sleeve, short for military police!

"Are you Hoan Tran?" he asked me in a booming voice!

"Yes, sir!" I answered, nervous and wondering what this was all about.

"You need to come with me down to the MP headquarters. We have to straighten something out!"

I didn't know much English but understood as he motioned for me to go with him, his expression cold and stern.

On the ride in his jeep down to the MP station, he didn't say one word, looking straight ahead and really freaking me out. After all, I was just a little kid. What could they possibly want with me?

I kept my eyes fixed on the road ahead, not daring to look sideways at him. I was taken to a room once we made it to the station. There were two other men in the room, one an older Asian man and the other an American MP.

"You know why you're here, son?" A middle-aged military police officer broke the silence, the older Asian man translating slowly in Vietnamese.

I did a double take, turning to the Asian man. "Did I do something wrong, sir?" I asked innocently since I had no clue what, if anything, I had done wrong.

"Were you walking around the open green fields collecting small white balls, washing them, and selling them back to the people around playing golf on these courses?" the man continued, the Asian man still translating.

"Yes, sir! I am. Am I not supposed to do that?" I asked truthfully, not knowing if anything was wrong with it.

"Son, as a refugee, and even if you are not, first, the area is off-limits to nonmilitary personnel, and second, no, you cannot collect those balls and sell them back. It's against the law," he said, looking directly at me, very serious. The Asian man, with the same expression, continued to slowly translate what was said into Vietnamese.

"No, sir! I did not know that. If I did, I wouldn't have done it!" I said, nervous and scared of what might happen.

"What do you think we should do with him, Phuc?" the man turned and asked the Asian man.

"We can lock him up for a few days to make sure he won't do it again," the Asian man answered.

I turned directly to the Asian man, speaking to him in Vietnamese, "I'm just a small boy, sir. I honestly didn't know I was not supposed to do that. You can't lock me up. I promise I won't do it again! I promise!" I looked from the Asian man to the military officer, a pleading expression written on my face.

After a few more minutes of deafening silence, both men busted out laughing at my expense. I felt a tinge of embarrassment and fear at the same time.

"We were just kidding with you, son, though it's true. The fields you were on are off-limits to nonmilitary personnel, and you cannot collect those golf balls and sell them back to the players. It's not allowed! But we know you didn't do it on purpose. We know you were just trying to make a little extra for your family. So we will forget it this time, but don't ever do it again!" the military officer finally told me, motioning to the other military officer to take me back to my building.

"Thank you, sir. I won't do it again!" I felt relieved, my stomach settling down a little as I followed the military officer who took me to the station back to the jeep.

For the next several months, life was uneventful. I dutifully performed my assigned role as the family supplier of stuff to get us through each and every day while awaiting to be picked up by a charity organization. The season changed. The camp was now in late fall, and leaves were turning beautifully red, orange, and yellow, reflecting the much more subdued mood I was feeling. I loved the colors of the trees changing, the leaves falling by the hundreds, each with its own distinct special characteristic, like each of us.

It had been eight months when the news finally came! We were going to Kansas City. Saint Francis Catholic Church agreed to sponsor our family. The wait was over! The temporary new life ended, giving way to what should be a more permanent new life, built in a new city among a real community and people, not in abandoned military bases serving as temporary housing. I felt an immense sense of relief. Finally, we could at least try to start our lives all over again. Welcome to America!

CHAPTER 17

Welcome to America!

I t was a snowy November afternoon. Looking through the window of the bus on a six-hour ride from Fort Chaffee, Arkansas, to Kansas City, Missouri, everything seemed so strange and sad. Empty field after empty field reflected the emotion I felt deep inside. I stared out at nothing in particular, as if just to have something to focus on but couldn't quite find it. Tears began welling up in my eyes, waiting for the chance to let loose. But I refused to let them. I sat with my head against the cold, foggy bus window, wishing I was anywhere else but here. The snow started falling harder and, in a matter of minutes, completely covered the street with wet white flakes. Even though the window was cold and frozen, I couldn't feel my head getting cold until I tried to pull it away, and strands of my hair were left behind. With some pain, I pulled myself away. Lying back against the headrest of my seat, I closed my eyes and immediately drifted into a deep sleep. My dad, brother, relatives, and friends—memories of my people rushing back to me; I wished I was there. The children selling lottery tickets on the crowded street corners, the beggars lining up on the busy side streets, the prostitutes along the dark alleys… I miss my *life*!

As the bus came to an abrupt stop in Kansas City, I broke out of my daydream and looked out the frosted window. Again I felt a great sense of loss, trying to adjust to the new surroundings! I remember telling myself, *Don't you dare pity yourself! You got work to do. You got people to worry about. You got your loved ones who love you and depend on you, even if they are not here.*

I fought back the tears as I stepped off the bus into the snowy, bitterly cold evening. It was the night before Thanksgiving.

I have plenty to be thankful for, I thought to myself. *I am still alive, so anything is possible.*

Looking out at the grounds covered in the cold white stuff, I knew what I had to do as my mind again drifted back to a much happier time.

In Vietnam, every day in a war zone was a struggle, fighting for every little necessity. Being alive the next day was not a guarantee. It was a privilege. But it was amazing how life went on as if nothing had happened. It had to! Otherwise, everyone would go insane thinking about what could happen!

The soccer field was rough, but no one minded. We were kids hungry to be outside, playing with friends. I was the smallest defenseman on the school soccer team. I was not quite athletic, but I was fast and just coordinated enough on my feet. Although, after many practice sessions and competitive games, I realized my strongest talent was giving up my body as a human shield. My sole responsibility was to protect the guy in front of the huge net, trying to prevent the ball from getting anywhere near him. Some days I could have stood there all day with nothing to do because our offense was so good, and the other side couldn't even recognize the ball even if it hit them in the face. On other days, I would be running for my life trying to catch up with the much faster kids from the other team, pushing the ball down to our side of the field at a maddening pace. Throughout my time as the defenseman on the team, I accumulated memorable bruises and scars to validate the job I did. I wore them proudly, as they represented my sense of duty, team spirit, and achievement. I believed then, and I still do now, that those bruises and scars were signs of growing up and a sense of never giving up, no matter how tough things got. We did fairly well as a soccer team, but obviously, I never went on to become the *soccer star* I dreamed of becoming, nor did any of my friends on the same team. But we were happy nonetheless!

A patch of the white stuff fell on my head, bringing me back to reality!

I scanned the white streets. The trees were bare, exposing the brittle brown branches, victims of the intense onset of winter. I was actually excited since this was the first time I saw snow in my life. I called it the cold white stuff! My feet froze as I stood there dazed, staring at everything. This, I later learned, was the housing project on the East Side.

I thought of my dad! He and I had a special relationship. He did not show his emotions openly toward me, but I always knew he was a very strong and kind man. He took great care of our family and constantly taught me about life and how to handle adversities. We had a routine every Sunday morning. He would take me to this famous noodle place, Pho Tau Bay, on his Vespa. Along the way, he would always tell me about life and how I should live when I grew up. This tradition started when I was eight years old. To be frank, I was always a little confused why he was telling me all the things he did when I was only eight years old. He would do this every Sunday on our way to the noodle shop until he passed away. He told me about the sense of duty, loyalty, honor, responsibility, pride, family, love, and of all things that matter to be a good person. He was absolutely right, as I later came to realize that all the things he told me was his way to prepare me for the fateful day when I had to leave my beloved birthplace to find freedom somewhere else. Of course, I was clueless until it happened! Sadly, it came much quicker than I imagined in my mind.

I traveled a great distance in the last few months, farther away from home. Everything was different and strange, and conditions were less than ideal, but we were refugees. Life changed forever the minute we left Vietnam. People were thrust together, not by choice but by fate. Scored one for human resilience, and life went on. I had more important things on my mind to notice the living conditions in these refugee camps. I would not allow the journey to freedom to be bothered by such trivialities. I did not pay attention to anything else, determined to adapt to my new life and make some friends along the way. I promised myself that. I felt a sense of uselessness and lack of purpose, totally dependent on others, even for food each day. I remembered that without my mom and my sisters, I was totally lost and useless when it came to feeding myself back home.

Knowing it would be a long while before we could make it out of the refugee camp, I devoted my time and effort to something more productive: running! I tried to run every day. It was more than keeping myself in shape. Maybe I wanted to run to escape from my own thoughts of what might have happened to my dad, my friends, and my life! Maybe I wanted to run to escape the everyday reminders of how far I was from home and how totally useless I was right now. I began reading anything I could get my hands on, even just looking at pictures if I could not understand the words, which was the sad truth. And so it went on!

Life in a refugee camp was not all bad. At first, I forced myself to make new friends with kids my age and their parents and siblings. But as time went by, I actually enjoyed this new chapter of my life. My new friends and I would walk the grounds, admiring the mountains and the hills.

Everything will be fine, I told myself, and for the most part, it was!

On and on it went for almost a year before the news came. We were selected by a Catholic church in Kansas City, Missouri, as part of their Rescue the Refugees Program. I was elated, although Kansas City, just like anything else about America, was totally foreign to me. Vietnam was an extremely isolated country, even from its own people sometimes. The news was fairly limited and controlled by the government. With very few exceptions, we could only hear what we were allowed to hear or given permission to hear. Truth was irrelevant. Only survival mattered! Laws seemed to be made up by the elite few in government as they went along. What applied today might not even be relevant or true tomorrow. It was hard for me to imagine that I once lived under those conditions and accepted them, maybe because I had no choice, or I was too young and ignorant to even realize it. I always wondered if I could have done something to make a difference after the war. I continue to question myself. I guess it's the "growing up" and "self-realization" parts of my life my dad spoke about so often to me during those Sunday trips to the noodle shop.

Still I had doubts about my self-worth, my place in the world, the "why am I here." Some of us were finally getting out of the refugee camp.

"Kansas City, here we come!"—even though I had no earthly idea where Kansas City was.

A big chunk of the white stuff that fell on my head from the tree above brought me back as I stood beside the bus that just dropped us off. I scanned the surroundings again with much more attention. I ventured along the sidewalks, not daring to walk too far. I saw Americans up close for the first time in my life. They all seemed taller and bigger than me. Of course, I was on the small side to start with. They were tall, with beautiful blue and green eyes and different skin colors, as I remembered. They looked at me cautiously since this was a new experience for them as well. I stared back at them with a smile, not knowing what else to do. They whispered something to each other that I could not understand. All I could do was stand there and smile. They broke out in a huge laugh, obviously enjoying their new pastime of making fun of the new, strange kid. But still I did not care. I smiled back and quietly walked along the snowy, slippery sidewalks to my assigned space.

I remember the house well, 417 Forest Street. The name sounded so romantic, yet it was anything but. It was a housing project in the worst part of the East Side of downtown Kansas City. The Missouri River running through it provided the illusion of something much more peaceful and grand than it actually was. I didn't care! I walked through the small door into the small place that was to be our new home for now! It was a place I later learned was called the project, situated in one of the poorest parts of Kansas City. But to me, it was a true blessing. While it seemed cold and dark, I tried to feel comfortable.

I thought of my dad, my brother, and my friends. We didn't have much back in Vietnam, but we had each other. The funny thing about the aftermath of a devastating event is that you don't seem to care about the materialistic things you lost. The love, friendships, and human bonds seemed to be much more important to me right now. Clinging to the thoughts of those warm nights in the comfort of family and friends kept me going. I looked around the empty room, tears coming down my face. I felt trapped. I shouldn't have been, but I was. For the first time, I felt as though I was in prison, even though I had found new freedom. I closed my eyes and collapsed on the floor. It felt cold but not as cold as I felt inside. I fell into a struggle to sleep from exhaustion until the light came through the windows the next morning.

I was truly alone in a place I didn't know. Again I thought of my family and friends. I managed to pull myself up from the floor. I needed to pull myself together. I needed an *attitude adjustment*!

I need to move on, I told myself.

Enough of this self-pity bullshit already! This was not what my dad had wanted me to become. He taught me better than this. I was better than this. I needed to start a new life, a better life. I thought of all the endless possibilities. I was becoming a man. Thinking about my dad, he had made it seem so easy to be a decent, caring, and kind person. I wondered if I would ever turn out to be even close to who he was. I smiled, knowing I still had dreams and people to care for. A new, bright life just began again for me, ironically in a cold, empty room. There was a lot to be thankful for and a lot of work to be done. After all, it was Thanksgiving Day!

CHAPTER 18

Fitting In

The first night in Kansas City, in a strange new place, was very difficult. I could not sleep. I was anxious, sad, worried, and homesick. The night couldn't move fast enough. I struggled to stay calm as the unknown completely consumed me. I tried to think good thoughts—of home, of friends, of places I came to know and love.

I opened the creaking old door, ready to explore my new neighborhood. The white stuff lined all the sidewalks, making it challenging to walk. I steadied myself, more emotionally than physically, as I plunged on, looking back to make sure I could mentally remember my way back. Ahead of my place was a huge playground with different luxuries—swing sets, a basketball court (I came to find out later), slides—all the stuff that made up kids' heaven. The white stuff made it seem abandoned, tired, and unattractive. The bitterly cold wind and the white stuff, I guessed at the time, kept people in their homes most of the time, unless they needed to go somewhere important. Cars lining the sides of the streets came in all sizes, shapes, and colors. I had never seen these many cars. In Vietnam, bikes and motorbikes made up almost 90 percent of all traffic, making it really chaotic and messy. I finally saw four kids playing outside, rolling up the white stuff and throwing it at one another. I saw kids of all ages, all shapes, all colors, talking and staring at me, curious, fascinated. I waved at them and smiled since my pitiful command of the English language rendered me absolutely useless in engaging in any small conversation, much less meaningful ones. They waved and smiled back. I realized one thing right then: as children, our capacity to see past the differences—skin color, age, and shape—was something we must never forget or give up. The four children, two with light skin and two with much darker skin, dived forward and rolled in the white stuff, seemingly unphased by the bitterly cold wind and laughing hysterically.

I cracked my own smile and told myself, *I will have time to get to know these kids, my neighbors. I have to become part of this community if I am to start my new life here.*

I walked across the empty white playground to a really tall old building on the other side. The sign read, "Garrison Community Center." It must have been there for a really long time. It had some broken windows, obviously had not been well-kept. I walked up the steps, pushing the heavy double doors to get inside. It was not much warmer, but there was no bitterly cold wind. All of a sudden, I felt very small and lost, standing now in the middle of the foyer. The old wooden floor cracked with splinters from people stomping all over it for years. I turned to my left. There was a full-size basketball court, with each side having a really tall pole with a basket hanging from it with no net. The floor continued from the foyer into this room; they were cracked and splintered just as badly. The top windows on the side were broken; small shards of glass were on the ground.

No one had played here for a while! I thought.

I let out a loud scream, and the room repeated my words instantly. I turned and walked out of the room to the other side of the foyer. A beautiful, ornate winding staircase leading to the next level occupied the entire right side of the foyer. I began climbing the staircase slowly, taking in the fascinating, meticulously carved railings, sadly splintered as the floor.

"What a shame!"

I admire historic landmarks and buildings of any kind. I imagined all the hard work that went into this stunning staircase and struggled to comprehend the neglect over the years! I would come to find out later that I was living in what some of my neighbors called the project, which was reserved for much lower-income families. But to me, this was where I got started with my new life in America, away from the destruction and atrocities. I struggled with the loneliness, the fear of the unknown, the strange new land, the strange new language, and the new people. But strangest of all, I was struggling with my newfound freedom. I stood at the top of the staircase, looking down the foyer, admiring the view, feeling insignificant, useless, lonely, and terrified. I fought hard not to cry, not to pity, not to worry, not to miss home, not to miss my family and friends, and not to miss my childhood. All these emotions were rushing through me like a tidal wave. I stood there, frozen, for what seemed to be an eternity.

The room at the top of the staircase was huge and engulfed me as I walked in. There was a ping-pong table with some cheap paddles at one end of the room. Crooked folding chairs lined one wall. There were some jump ropes and a badly damaged billiard table with the surface cloth torn up and crooked cue sticks. All this barely made a dent in the huge space of this room. I walked over to the ping-pong table.

"Finally, something I can recognize!"

I smiled as I picked up the damaged blue paddle and realized there was no ball. Dejected, I walked over to the billiard table and examined the cue sticks. They were as badly damaged as the table's surface. I walked slowly out of the room with the intention to come back soon and maybe meet and make new friends.

"Welcome to America!" I whispered to myself, descending down the staircase and plunging into the bitterly cold wind again.

The church car pulled up, and the deacon, Geremiah, knocked on my door, waking me up from a night of struggling to sleep. Knowing my nonexistent command of the English language, he tried very hard to communicate, always with a soft, gentle smile on his face! He was assigned several of the people brought to Kansas City on that bus, and I was one of them. He brought extra toothpaste, toothbrushes, soap, shampoo—everyday grooming luxuries.

"It's time for Sunday Thanksgiving Mass!" he said gently, pulling out a picture of the church (Saint Francis's Catholic Church) and making a praying gesture with his hands!

I understood but wondered if he realized I was not Catholic. But I came to learn that going to Mass was a strong requirement for all the incoming immigrants, or refugees, as we were called. I quickly put on my shorts and T-shirt I brought along from Vietnam for the long trip. I was the only one in the family to represent us at church! Geremiah laughed as he looked at me, then outside, where the white stuff continued to fall. Geremiah was very tall—well over six feet tall—donning a long, heavy coat. He came prepared and handed me a jacket and long pants. I looked back at him, thankful. At least I knew how to say thank you. I quickly put on the long pants and jacket as we headed to his car! It was quite a long car—a four-door, bright-yellow sedan belonging to the church. I settled in the back seat as Geremiah made a couple more stops to pick up the rest of the people he was responsible for.

Geremiah waved and shouted hello to another deacon driving up in a white van with the church's name on the side. "Good morning, Dennis! How are you?" Geremiah called out in a wide, full smile.

"Hey, Geremiah! I am good. How about you? What a beautiful day! You gotta love this!" Dennis smiled back. He was also very tall, well over six feet. He was also on his way to pick up the other families he was assigned for Thanksgiving Mass.

All of us were put in different houses but in the same approximate neighborhood. I didn't get a chance to meet and get to know the other families on the bus ride to Kansas City since I was too busy thinking and falling in and out of sleep. I represent my family as the non-Catholic contingent going to church. This was one of the rules: at least one member of the family would need to go to church at assigned times. It seemed every other family was Catholic except ours. I looked about the white grounds, the soft powder falling effortlessly, the wind swaying the dried branches of the bare trees! This seemed fitting, given my feelings at the time: empty and cold.

After the friendly greetings, Geremiah climbed into the car and started to head slowly forward. The blast of warm air from the heater caught me by surprise, but it was much needed. Geremiah looked back at me from the rearview mirror of the car as I stared out the window, still trying to comprehend and struggling to accept the new reality.

I will get there eventually! I told myself, curling up in my seat.

Geremiah took only a couple minutes before he got out and knocked on another door in the neighborhood, picking up the next family! A woman and her two children walked slowly to the car, being careful not to slip on the white stuff. She was an older lady, probably in her fifties, and her two sons were in their late thirties. They also settled in the back seat, with the mother next to me.

"My name is Hoan! Very nice to meet you!" I said hello with a soft smile. I was used to being friendly since my encounters with several different families on the bus.

"I am Hoa, and these are my children, Quang and Tam!" The mother smiled as she answered. Her sons nodded toward me with a soft hello.

I could tell they were Catholics, with Hoa holding a long black rosary, running her fingers along the beads. I saw that before in Vietnam when people prayed! I felt a little out of place being the only non-Catholic so far in the car. Geremiah seemed to realize this and nodded at me with a wide smile, trying to put me at ease! He pulled up to the last stop, picking up a younger mother and daughter. She was in her thirties, and her daughter was in her late teens. They, too, walked gently toward the car, being careful not to slide on the slick white surface. They got into the front seat of the car. She reminded me of the older version of Lan, the young lady and her son I met on the plane on the way here!

"Hi, I am Hoan. Nice to meet you!" Again I was the first one to speak up.

"I am Van, and this is my daughter, Mai! Nice to meet you too!" She said cheerfully as she turned her head toward us in the back seat.

"And this is Hoa, Quang, and Tam!" I boldly took the lead in introducing the people sitting next to me, not bothering to ask them if it was okay with them. Thinking back, I was a little embarrassed, but since they seemed fine with it, it made me feel much better.

We largely stayed quiet the rest of the trip to Saint Francis, taking roughly thirty minutes from where we were because of the white stuff making the streets very slick. Geremiah tried his best to talk to us, saying things we absolutely could not understand. But we listened intently.

This is what patience looks like, I thought to myself, *something I got to have much more of if I am to integrate myself into my new reality and environment!*

The white stuff was quite blinding as the car moved at constant speed forward, passing along the bare trees. I thought of home again, my mind drifting.

The beautiful oak trees lining the middle of one of the busiest streets in Vietnam, Nguyen Hue Street (named after one of the most famous kings in Vietnam), mesmerized both locals and tourists alike. Motorbikes, bicycles, and the occasional automobile moved painfully slow through the crowded street, with people moving and crossing constantly among the many shops along the sidewalks. The smell of the different Vietnamese favorite foods drew large crowds every single minute of the day, rain or shine! The souvenir shops rang with the loud voices of the owners advertising their merchandise to tourists willing to pay top money for souvenirs of all sorts to mark their presence in Vietnam.

My favorite thing to do had always been to visit the many bookstores along this street to satisfy my love of reading. My friends and I would spend a lot of our free time on the weekend on this street, especially in the evenings when bright lights lit up the trees. Stores blended with people talking and laughing. But underneath the happy, glamorous surface was the devastating truth of war. Just as there were many tourists and locals with money, there were also people living in poverty—the beggars, the hungry children, the lottery ticket peddlers, the prostitutes—making this famous street as much of an attraction as it was one of the worst slums in Vietnam. Life moved simultaneously and seamlessly between two opposite worlds! I often wondered what it would be like without the war I had known all my years there! I remember the loud sirens warning of possible bombings close to the capital city. All of us were well-conditioned to go immediately into hideouts or shelters in our homes or wherever we were at the time. But no one seemed to worry whether they would live through each day with how they went about their day. They were too busy working to feed their families and put their children through school—all the typical things families would do each and every day. They laughed, they cried, they argued, and they loved! Their lives moved along as they would each and every day for years! We had all been very well-conditioned, indeed. I tried hard not to become numb to this well-conditioned life.

This is how the spirit dies, I thought to myself.

While my dad fought hard to keep our country and our family safe, I was fighting to keep my spirit and my hope alive. I couldn't afford to see my dad's fighting effort wasted.

"We're here!" Geremiah's voice brought me back.

We were in front of an old but majestic church. Peeking out from the car window, I saw the gigantic, rustic church bell on the rooftop of the church that gave it a historical, almost mystic, look, straight out of a mystery novel. I had never seen anything like it, even with the many churches I saw in Vietnam. Geremiah cracked a gentle smile, watching my astonished expression at the grand church bell.

He opened the car doors for everyone, carefully helping the ladies out of the car! I put my feet slowly outside the car, planting them on the ground as if expecting it to sink. The breeze was refreshing but cold as I took in a much-needed deep breath. My body struggled to adapt, not used to being exposed to this extreme cold. I tried to act tough, refusing to shiver.

Saint Francis was a grand old church sitting in the middle of a huge lot with trees all around. I took a quick peek at the courtyard on the side, with a beautiful fountain dripping peacefully on a freezing morning. This, while foreign to me, somehow gave me a sense of peace and comfort. I took in the serene surroundings, the fresh air, the uncertainty, the fear, and the anxiety! Everything jumbled in my small head, thousands of miles away from home.

It's so quiet, scary quiet!

It occurred to me that there were no bombs, no sirens, no beggars, no lottery ticket peddlers, no prostitutes, no sidewalk food vendors, and no souvenir shops. It was completely devoid of the many things I was so used to. A sense of desperation and profound sadness washed over me. I stood still, as frozen as the ground that morning, feeling just as cold as the white stuff. Tears came to my eyes again without any provocation. I clenched my fist, quietly and secretly vowing I would have to build a new life here, as strange and uncomfortable as it was.

Geremiah came over and put his hand on my shoulder, worry in his eyes! "It will all be okay!" he whispered softly, but obviously, I did not understand at the time.

Geremiah gathered his crew and led them on to the church steps. They seemed to go on forever! After a few minutes, we were in front of some massive, highly ornate doors. Geremiah pushed them open slowly and gestured for us to go inside! The brightly lit candles warmed this absolutely stunning church, with picture glass on the big windows along the walls. All the pews were neatly and orderly arranged in three separate rows, with the walkway lined with red carpet. I looked forward to the circular main altar with a long table covered in white cloth with a golden cross prominently displayed on the front. On the back wall, a huge wooden cross with purple cloth draped over it signified the crucifixion of Christ. I looked in awe, having no real knowledge of Catholicism since I was raised a Buddhist. I tried my best to blend into the new Catholic environment, as if being in a completely strange country and not knowing the people, the culture, or the language were not challenging enough. I smiled to myself secretly, wondering what else would come along on this exhausting journey that would render me in awe.

I decided to follow Geremiah's lead as he guided us toward the front pews. We must have been early since there was no one else in the church. After a few moments, Dennis, the other deacon I saw earlier in our hood, walked his herd toward the front of the church. I looked more observantly at all the people—the same people who took the bus ride with me from Fort Chaffee, Arkansas! They looked thankful but so sad! I could see with the older people that it seemed more dramatic for them, probably leaving the only place they had known all their lives. While they had some family with them, which was much more than I can say for myself, I was sure they left behind many, many loved ones. There was a story behind each and every one of those faces, kids and adults alike!

An idea popped into my disturbed head; I would take the lead in getting to know each and every one of them in the coming days, weeks, and months! I turned and looked straight at the altar, settling into the edge of the second pew in the middle row. I sat down, realizing how small I was, even in this church, much less in the grand universe. I miss *home*! I miss my friends! I miss my life! Wiping a quick tear from my eyes, I immediately came to my senses. This was my life now. Like it or not, I got to get over this pity feeling and get on with my new life! I promised myself things would get better; I would get better! I sat in silence and enjoyed the peaceful feeling inside me. Life would get better! I smiled!

CHAPTER 19

Family Away from Family

More people of all ages filled the church pews. They all looked strange to me. I had never seen anyone with skin and hair colors different than mine, not even on television. Hair of different colors—gray, silver, brown, and gold—lined the church pews. Before I could let my thoughts stray further, a towering figure walked onto the altar, his hair as white as the white stuff outside. He wore a white robe with a beautiful purple scarf draped around and hanging elegantly in the front, a golden cross and a white dove on each side. His face was peaceful, his smile brilliant, and his facial complexion rosy. He stopped in the middle of the altar, his hands on the huge table. Flanking on both sides of the altar table were four young boys, maybe about my age, also in simple white robes, again with hair of different colors! I would later find out he was Father Flannagan, the head of the diocese. He began speaking, praying, as the congregation repeated after him in a strange language I would later try very hard to master. But at the time, I just stood in silence, eyes closed as if praying, hiding the fact that my thoughts were once again drifting toward a place far, far away. I was home again!

*****

The street was busy and noisy, with loud voices and kids running disorderly. The shops were crowded with shoppers as my friends and I made it to the heart of the tourist district! We were excited for another new year to come, with hopes of a more peaceful and less eventful year. I couldn't remember how often my friends and I had the same wish over the years, but it didn't seem to come true as of yet. But that didn't stop us from making the same wish this year, or should we say, "wishful thinking!" For folks like us, living in a war-torn country all our lives (well, young lives like us), hope was all we got, really. So wish away we did, over and over again!

Diep and I biked together to the city center, meeting up with the rest of our group. We had our designated spot; otherwise, it would be almost impossible to find people in this madness. Diep and I were the first at the Nguyen Hue bookstore, our rendezvous spot. The bookstore was tightly packed with people, young and old, students, and families. After all, it was the weekend, the only time people have to unwind. Our group finally caught up with us, smiling as they greeted us.

"It was so crowded, making it almost impossible to bike myself here!" Nhat complained.

"Yea! Sorry, guys. I was stopped at every single traffic light known to men!" Thao chimed in.

"Crybabies!" Lan laughed as she spoke up since she beat both Nhat and Thao to the rendezvous spot.

"You guys want to head to the cathedral?" I, the organizer, took the lead.

"Yup! It should be so beautiful now. They always do a great job decorating and lighting the trees and the courtyard," Diep answered, beaming.

We jumped on our bikes and started pedaling toward the west side of Nguyen Hue Street. The entire street was plugged up with thousands upon thousands of people. But we loved this inconvenience and noise. It gave us a strange sense of security and comfort, a calm sense of "normalcy," and a joyful sense of "childhood." The smell of the street food vendors and the sight of people holding hands, laughing, and talking painted a stunning picture of what it all should be. For the first time in a long time, I smiled to myself, thankful for these wonderful moments, lasting memories, and enduring friendships! We biked, the wind in our faces, toward the city center cathedral.

We loved it here at Christmastime and hated it most at the same time. The scene was so majestic, but we spent a lot of time and effort bobbing and weaving through a sea of people. We were literally packing on top of each other with absolutely no daylight between us. I could feel Diep's breath on my neck, literally. Well, at least it was not some stranger's breath. We tried to stay very close to one another; otherwise, it would be impossible to look for anyone in this absolute mess. Somehow, I felt a sense of peace deep within me. I knew I belonged here! I knew this is where I wanted to be—the good, the bad, and the ugly. I welcomed it all. But today, it was all beauty, all elegance, all peace, all love—all home!

*****

"Amen!" the congregation said in unison, waking me from my brief encounter with my past.

I stole a look around the church. Everyone was still very attentive, an expression of gratefulness painted across the faces of the worshippers! I stood in silence, as I had the whole time since this Thanksgiving Mass started, staring deeply at each of the worshippers in the church. They were in a trancelike state, rocking their bodies gently back and forth. I wished I could jump back into my memories and take another long walk down *childhood memory lane*. As a young boy, my attention span was quite limited on most things, to start with, much less for a very lengthy ceremony I had absolutely no idea about. And it had been a really long time, according to the internal time clock! I nodded in and out of consciousness throughout the ceremony and somehow didn't feel so bad about it.

The young altar boys walked toward the front, one on each side of Father Flannagan, as they walked toward the bottom step of the altar. Two of the worshipers moved forward, one holding a small crystal bottle with some red liquid in it and the other holding a round brass box. As they approached the front of the steps, they handed each of the items to each of the altar boys. Father Flannagan made the cross sign as they bowed their heads and quietly mumbled, "Amen," then walked back to their seats. I later found out from Geremiah, with a lot of sign language and drawing pictures, that they were asking for special ceremony prayers from the congregation for one of their passing family members! I felt a tinge of guilt for nodding off during the whole mass.

So disrespectful! I thought.

From that day on, I was on much better behavior during mass. As part of the sponsorship, we would attend masses on Mondays, Wednesdays, Fridays, and Sundays. I was the only non-Catholic in the entire refugee clan, and I felt really out of place most of the time. Geremiah did his best to make sure I didn't get down too much about it. After mass, Geremiah and Dennis gathered their respective crews and headed down to the courtyard next door. We were guided to the small building on the side of the church. Geremiah said it was the "catch all" building where the kitchen and cafeteria, some classrooms, some storage rooms, and the television room where the priests, nuns, deacons, and volunteer staff gather to do their work for the community and prepare for Mass were located. Geremiah said that on Sundays, the entire congregation would bring food and drinks to celebrate with each other after Mass to bring the community together. I looked at all the food on the tables. I had never seen so much food in my life! My eyes were as big as watermelons, and my stomach was growling. Geremiah noticed and cracked a wide smile, his teeth as white as the white stuff on the ground! He felt pity for me, I was guessing, being all alone when everyone else had families with them.

As the entire congregation gathered inside the hall cafeteria, Father Flannagan walked in, his face still rose pink and so peaceful. Apparently, he would "bless" the food before we could eat. Everyone lowered their heads, hands clasped, as Father Flannagan started the prayers, saying thanks for the blessing of the foods. And at the end, everyone said in unison, "Amen."

Father Flannagan smiled widely and told everyone, "Let's eat! I am hungry!"

Geremiah told me to grab a plate and follow him as he made his way orderly to each of the stations along the long row of tables. As he stopped at each station, he turned to me and said, "Take what you want and need and put it on your plate."

I struggled to understand, but from his hand gestures, I somewhat got the idea. I gestured back to Geremiah. *Everything? On the same plate?*

He smiled and nodded. I nodded back as he said, "You can come back later and get more!"—of course, with some added hand signs. I smiled broadly, full of anticipation.

I stopped at the chicken station first, the beautiful drumsticks and thighs—my favorite meat, dark! I took one of each and put them on my plate! The next station was good old mashed potatoes, I was told! I put a scoop on my plate, skipping the weird brown stuff that was supposed to go on top of it. The next station was salad, as I recognized the lettuce, tomatoes, and cucumbers. I hesitated at the dressing next to the salad. Geremiah tried his best to explain, helping me decide which I would like best! I settled for the vinaigrette since it was the simplest.

And who wouldn't like vinegar? I thought.

I continued walking down the long table, stopping at the bread station. Many different breads of different shapes smelled so wonderful. I temporarily froze, not able to decide which bread I liked. I finally settled on two rolls, one soft and one hard! As I stopped in front of all the desserts—cakes and pudding—Geremiah signaled me to go find a seat, and we could come back later for deserts! I smiled embarrassingly and followed him. I picked a seat next to Van and her daughter, Mai, so I could at least speak Vietnamese for a little while! Geremiah on my other side smiled and nodded, seemingly understanding the situation.

"So how did you sleep last night?" I started the conversation.

"Not well. It's so strange here!" Van spoke first, with Mai looking on in silence.

Mai was about the same age as I was; I was guessing. She was very shy and didn't seem to talk much. She kept her head down, looking at her plate of food, mostly salads and a small soft roll. There was a sadness on her face, her fingers swirling constantly in circles!

She must be thinking about something back home, just like I did from time to time, I thought!

"She is having a really hard time, Hoan," Van confided in me. "She misses her relatives, but most of all, she misses her friends. I told her she will get used to it and build a new life here. She will come around to it."

"I know the feeling!" I confessed to them. "If you like, we can be friends!" I told Mai, who was still looking down at her plate. "I live on 417 Forest Street, right in front of the play yard and community center. Where do you guys live?" I tried to cheer them up.

"We are at 729 Sycamore Street. I think we are a couple rows of houses from you," Van answered, smiling a little now.

"Great. I will try to come over sometimes and say hello," I promised them.

I thought I saw Mai cracking a little smile out of one corner of her mouth as she started to get into her food! We sat in silence as we started eating. I looked over to my other side.

Geremiah nodded happily, smiling as if to say, "You all will be okay!"

I picked up my chicken leg and took a huge bite out of it, as if I had been starving for days. In Vietnam, chicken was considered fairly valuable and would cost a little more money to get. So for most of the poor families, they wouldn't be able to afford to eat chicken except once in a very long while! I started chewing slowly, my mind drifting back to my beloved neighborhood.

*****

Children were running everywhere, screaming as they played some of their favorite games like hide-and-seek and hop the squares. There were a couple of food vendors, with their carts full of steaming good food. Diep and I were walking along the small alley close to our homes, taking in the aroma of the wonderful food. We nodded and decided to eat Vietnamese rice rolls today. We were regulars. As the lady saw us coming, she pulled out two small, low chairs for us to sit.

"Com'on, boys! The usual?" she said cheerfully.

"Yes, ma'am," we said in unison as we laughed.

She expertly poured the flour onto her big, round pan with such precision. She covered the lid briefly for the rice roll to take shape! After a few seconds, she opened the lid, started spreading the ground pork and mushroom, and rolled up the rice paper! It was amazing to see how she was able to turn out exactly the same-looking rice roll every single time! She cut the long roll into smaller pieces on the plate, putting mint, cilantro, roasted dried onion, bean sprouts, and thinly diced cucumber and topping it off with spicy, sweetened fish sauce.

"Dig in, boys!" she proudly told us, smiling broadly. She told us often that the best thing anyone could do to make her happy was to eat her food honestly, enjoy it fully, and keep coming back—and come back we did almost every other morning, whether it was a regular weekday or on the weekend. Our mouths watered just looking at it. We ate as if the world was coming to an end, without uttering one word!

*****

A gentle tap on my shoulder brought me back. Geremiah, smiling, signaled me to get back up to the table for some desserts. I got to get out of these trips back to memory lane. They happened at the worst time and were getting out of control, putting me in embarrassing situations. I stood up and started walking toward the dessert station. The chocolate cookies looked great, and I grabbed a couple onto my plate. Geremiah tried to explain that all the food was made by the people in the congregation, taking turns from week to week. I caught the sight of a nun, who was just as tall as Geremiah, as she waved at me, smiling peacefully. She had a long face, and the veil and coif made her face look even longer. Her soft and gentle eyes, with a big pair of glasses, were full of joy and peace!

"That's Sister Claire. She is one of the six nuns in the convent next door. She comes every week to help Father Flannagan prepare for the services. She also teaches English to the children of the congregation. By the way, she will be teaching you and the others English at this building starting next week," Geremiah said in a long breath.

Seeing the bewildered look on my face, he smiled. But I got the meaning of "Sister Claire," "teaching," "English," and "you and others" enough to know I would soon learn English from her. I nodded to Geremiah, letting him know I understood. Geremiah began gathering his crew again, telling us we were heading home for the day.

But before we headed out, Father Flannagan told Geremiah and Dennis to take all of us down to the basement. They led us through a small hallway, opening the creaky door to the basement. I realized these buildings, the main church included, had been there a long time, with time and the weather beating on them through the seasons of extreme heat and cold. It did not seem as though Father Flannagan and the congregation were able to do much to keep up with the fixes, both minor and major. I could tell the neighborhood where the church and the congregation reside was average financially, at best. I learned from Geremiah and Dennis that they were mostly of Italian descent. I remembered during the Mass today that baskets were passed around for collections. I guessed they used the money for any necessary repairs but also for food for the church staff.

Geremiah turned on the light as we headed down a narrow stairway to the basement. I felt a creepy sensation, as if something would suddenly jump out at any minute and grab us by the neck. I kept looking over my shoulder, only to see the other refugees in my clan. I smiled sheepishly as I continued down the stairs. Geremiah took a right turn into a bigger area, turning on the lights as we moved along. We finally stopped in front of a big table with a mountain of clothes piled high toward the ceiling—pants in one pile, shirts and blouses in the next, and shoes on the end.

Geremiah and Dennis started telling us, "Father Flannagan would like each of you to pick out three items of each and a pair of shoes. These shoes should help with the cold winter ahead of us. These are donations from the congregation and might not be a perfect fit for you. But this is all we can do, so pick the ones that would fit you best!"

Again the only thing I understood were "three of each," since they were accompanied by Geremiah and Dennis raising three fingers! We all nodded.

"What did they say?" Van whispered to me, and I smiled.

"They said each of us should take three of each item and a pair of shoes for the winter. These were donated by the congregation, so they might not be a great fit, but do what we can," I told Van, and she nodded.

I was still very small at the time, and finding pants that fit would be difficult. I didn't even pay attention to the appearance but rather focused on things that fit. I measured the pants by stretching them in front of me for width and length. The pair of pants that caught my eye were white, with zigzag red lines running the entire length. I picked it up, admiring it.

Very interesting! Loud, but interesting! I thought to myself as I decided to take it.

Out of the corner of my eyes, Mai was laughing quietly at my awful choice. For shirts, I obviously decided on all long-sleeved and one sweater I thought would keep me extremely warm. Moving down to the shoe line, I settled for a fake pair of white boots with just-above-ankle height.

"Put the shoes on!" Geremiah told me.

"Now?" I asked.

"Why not!" he answered.

I took off my regular, thin shoes and put on the fake white boots. Luckily, they fit perfectly.

"Looks great!" Geremiah said, smiling.

I looked over at the rest of our extended refugee family! Everyone was still rummaging through the three piles of stuff. A sense of sadness ran through me as I drifted off again.

*****

The street was busy with shoppers, buying and bargaining for stuff, crowding into small spaces. The noise was deafening! Diep, Thao, and I didn't need anything in particular. We liked to walk and "people watch." We stopped in front of the T-shirt shop, with rows after rows of T-shirts hanging from the rack of the homemade wooden stand. T-shirts of all colors and designs printed on them blinded me. Thao was the "fashion expert" in our group, although a little conservative for my taste. I liked bright colors—very bright colors! I assumed this had to do with how I looked at the world! Living in a war-torn country where *destruction and devastation* were the only constants, I wanted to have colors in my life, in the world! I told only Diep my thoughts on it since he was my best friend! He understood, but he, too, was on the conservative side for my taste.

"This one looks so good!" I told Diep and Thao, pointing at the bright-yellow T-shirt with a dragon on it. Dragons were my favorite mythology animal; they were so majestic, so elegant, and so powerful.

Diep and Thao let out a loud laugh, holding their stomachs with their hands.

"What's wrong with it?" I asked, resentful.

"Nothing!" Diep tried hard to answer through his laugh.

"That's definitely you!" Thao said sarcastically.

"Well, you guys know nothing about fashion!" I said defiantly.

"Are you going to get it?" Diep looked at me.

"I will think about it!" I said, walking away as they snickered softly behind me.

*****

A nudge on my arm brought me back again.

Geremiah whispered, "Time to go!"

I walked briskly, joining the group that was already at the bottom staircase. The warmth inside this building made me dread going outside to the cold and more white stuff. I clenched my fist, bracing for the wind blowing bitterly cold air on my face on the way to the car! I readied myself as I bolted to a full sprint toward the car, with

Geremiah already by the side of the car, holding the door open for me. I smiled as I jumped quickly inside.

It's all going to be alright! For the first time, I felt an uplift in my spirit. *It's all going to be alright!* I repeated it in my head as the car slowly rolled out to the street, rolling over the white, crunchy stuff, heading back to my new private place.

The sky turned darker, the wind howled stronger, and the cold got more bitter as I looked out the car window, smiling.

CHAPTER 20

"Can You Help me?"—
First English Lesson

A brown station wagon pulled up outside my place, and Sister Claire stepped out in full light-gray nun gear—the long robe, coif, and veil. She looked very elegant and peaceful. Every time I looked at Sister Claire, a sense of calmness and inner peace came over me. Her smile, which was so gentle, and her eyes, soft and caring, told me she lived a life of service and dedication to helping people.

She knocked on my door as softly as her eyes!

I opened the door, able to at least say, "Good morning, Sister!"

"How are you today, Hoan?" She was the first one to actually say my name exactly the way it should sound.

"I am fine. How are you?" I answered in the exact way I was taught English in Vietnam, afraid to sway away from it and risking Sister Claire not being able to understand what I was saying.

"Good. We are picking up some more people and heading to the church for our first English class today!" she said gently as I closed the apartment door, following her to the car!

I picked the same back seat as the one I took in Geremiah's car. Sister Claire gave a thumbs-up as she started rolling her station wagon slowly down the street. I assumed she would pick up Van and Mai next since they were the next stop on our last trip with Geremiah. As the car came to a stop, I could see the "729 Sycamore" address and knew Van and Mai would be the next ones to come to

158

the car! They made their way to the car, and we exchanged the usual greetings. Sister Claire picked up one more family, having the same crew responsibility as Geremiah. Soon the car proceeded slowly and cautiously through the now-hardened streets lined with ice and more white stuff. Sister Claire made the cross sign before heading out to the street, a gesture I came to understand she always performed prior to doing anything, asking for blessings!

It was very hard to recognize all the streets on the way to church with all the white stuff covering the streets, the signs, and the roads. I looked out of Sister Claire's car window as I had the day before, riding with Geremiah, not feeling as isolated as yesterday. Things were a lot quieter here than in Vietnam, regardless of what time of day it was. It was something I struggled to get used to in my first few days here. Being around Sister Claire, though, I felt a stronger sense of calm and peace. She focused on the road ahead; her face remained peaceful. The streets were devoid of people, and the fields were wide open with no houses or buildings on them. After what seemed to take a lot longer than it should, Sister Claire parked her car on the street in front of the church's courtyard! I opened the door, stepping out one foot at a time.

"Be careful, Hoan! It's very slippery!" she cautioned me, walking to the other side to let Van and Mai out of the back seats. Hoa and her two sons, Quang and Tam, opened the front door of the building, stepping out into the cold. Sister Claire caught up with the other crew, this time guided by Sister Theresa instead of Dennis, in front of the courtyard building.

"Good morning, Sister Theresa!" Sister Claire said softly, slightly bowing her head.

Sister Theresa was much older than Sister Claire! She must be in her sixties. Sister Claire later told me Sister Theresa was the head nun and head master of the church's Catholic school. She was much shorter than Sister Claire and full of life. I was excited to finally be doing something different to get my mind off my imaginary trips back to Vietnam.

Once inside the courtyard building, the sisters took us through the cafeteria we ate at yesterday after Mass into a long hallway. They took a left turn and led us into a big classroom with tables and chairs already set up—a total of six tables, each with five chairs in two equally arranged rows! I headed toward the front of the classroom, sitting on the end of the first table, anxious to get started! On the tables, thick English books, small notebooks, pens, and pencils were arranged in a very orderly fashion. We were all ready to start. Sister Claire headed to the front of the classroom, where a table and chair were situated in the middle, not much different from the teacher's desk in Vietnam. She formally wrote her name on the chalkboard.

"I am Sister Claire, for those who have not met me yesterday. I will be teaching you English for the next few months! This is a little different from the regular English classes. We will focus on what is necessary for you to carry on everyday conversations," she said to the bewildered look of all the new students in the room. But she pressed on.

"This is the first time we have such a class and the first time I teach this class in this way. We will learn together!" She smiled gently, looking at each of the new students with much hope and anticipation. "It will be a lot of fun and helpful. You might not be able to understand anything I am saying right now, but in time, hopefully, you will be able not only to understand what I am saying but to talk to me just as you talk Vietnamese to each other!" Her voice was filled with optimism and pride.

Sister Claire reminded me a lot of my literature teacher, Miss Lan, from her demeanor, her calm and peaceful face, her elegant walk, and her soft and gentle voice, except she was a lot taller and a nun. I began to feel a temporary sense of belonging, learning English three days a week, the same days we would attend Mass for the sake of convenient transportation. Sister Claire would pick us up on Monday, Wednesday, and Friday mornings for our lessons, and Geremiah would take us home after Mass. Being in the same place with the same group of people gave me a sense of familiarity and security. Too many changes had happened over the last year. It was time for some normalcy and calmness. But I knew, things would only get more difficult from here! It was time for me to grow up—and fast. I looked around the room and smiled. Everyone, while so different from one another, carried the same burden and emotional baggage of leaving behind our homes, our families, our friends, and our lives—all in the name of freedom. As much as life was precious, freedom—to me and, I am sure, to the others—was much more precious.

"Hoan, are you okay?" Sister Claire called out, realizing I was beginning to drift off.

"Yes, Sister!" I refocused on the lesson at hand.

Sister Claire was a professional English teacher. She gave us a syllabus for the class, divided into three major categories: reading, writing, and listening. She told us not to worry about right or wrong but to really put ourselves out there and speak up as loudly and confidently as we could. I noticed the older members of our class were more reserved and shy. This was the personality trait of most elderly people in Vietnam, the "do not speak unless you are spoken to" mindset. Sister Claire showed her true passion for teaching, very patient at every turn, regardless of how challenging the situation was.

We would have two hours of listening to start the class, then reading for the next two hours, and finishing up with writing for the last two hours, each with a thirty-minute snack break in between. I could tell everyone in the class really enjoyed Sister Claire and her class. She made our lessons very lively, showing some clips in between the book lessons. Just like in a regular English class, we had to take quizzes along the way and an exam at the end to assess our understanding of the lessons. While learning English was a challenge, to be sure, it was the least difficult thing I had to face coming to America. There were things ahead that would take all my energy, effort, and passion to get through to be a part of this new home and new world! I promised myself at that moment that I would make the most of the opportunity given. I focused on Sister Claire's lesson. A smile came to me as I really began to start my new life!

CHAPTER 21

The American Dream

After two weeks, I settled down in my new home, doing my best to organize my life. It was time to make some money to manage my small expenses! It was time to work on the American Dream, one small step at a time.

Geremiah came one Tuesday morning to help me apply for work, with the blessings of Father Flannagan. Finding work for a young boy with a very weak command of the English language and no life skills to speak of was a tall order for anyone. Geremiah was not just anyone. He was very special, having migrated to America at a young age as well. On the ride that day to help me look for work, Geremiah opened up about his life and his family for the first time since I landed in Kansas City, although I could not understand much of what he was saying! But I listened intently as he slowed down his speech considerably to accommodate my minimal grasp of the conversation.

He came from Africa—Ethiopia, to be exact. He made his way to America by himself, with the help of the Catholic Church. He did not go into real details about his journey, but I could tell he was emotionally affected by the ordeal. He came from a single-parent home, with his mother taking care of him and his two siblings, one boy and one girl, both younger than him. When he was back in his homeland, he felt the calling of the Catholic Church at a young age and went to seminary school in Ethiopia. While a large population of Ethiopians were Christians, only a very small percentage were Catholic. Geremiah told me there was always a distrust for the Catholic faith. Geremiah told me he left Ethiopia with the help of a Catholic priest who was on a mission in Ethiopia and settled in Kansas City, under the guidance of Father Flannagan, studying theology at Rockhurst College, a well-known Jesuit college in Kansas City. Father Flannagan and Saint Francis Church sent all their deacons to Rockhurst College to strengthen their theology, focus, and understanding. I could tell Geremiah still struggled with memories of his home and his family. Every time we talked about our families in my terribly broken English, he would tear up from time to time. He told me it had been a long time since he opened up about his personal life, and it brought back a lot of memories, good and bad. We sat in silence for the rest of the trip to my new potential place of work! He told me we were in the center of downtown Kansas City. I guessed that much since we were surrounded by tall, fancy buildings, something I was not used to in Vietnam. Geremiah smiled as I scanned around in awe.

He finally parked in front of what looked like a restaurant to me, but the pictures on the windows were very strange, of foods I didn't recognize. Geremiah let out a big laugh as my expression soured. We got out of the car, braving the cold wind that froze the awkward look on my face!

"This is Wendy's. They sell what's called fast food here in America. And these are hamburgers," he said, pointing at the drawings on the window as we walked inside the restaurant, stomping our feet on the entrance mat to shake off the snow on our shoes! I was quite fond of my new, fake white boots. They didn't seem to keep out the cold, with water seeping through, making my socks quite wet and freezing my toes. Geremiah got on more massive, thick boots.

"Are you cold?" he asked gently.

"I am okay!" I tried to act tough, even though I couldn't feel my toes, which were totally frozen stiff at the time.

"We will wait for these couple of customers to order, then we can go up!" he informed me of our plan.

The customers in front of us rattled off a whole bunch of words, with the young girl frantically marking off her order pad. I assumed she was part of the staff since she had a red apron with the word "Wendy's" prominently displayed on it and a picture of a smiling little girl in pigtails. She was smiling as required as she greeted each customer, gently saying thank you after each order! Geremiah and I were up next after the last customers were taken care of. Luckily, there was no one else in line behind us.

"Can we talk to the manager, please?" Geremiah told the young girl.

"Sure! Can you wait over there? I will let him know you want to see him," she said, smiling, although we didn't buy anything to be considered a "real" customer!

"Thank you," Geremiah said, displaying his most valuable asset, his smile.

We headed to the side of the dining area. Customers were sitting at different tables and booths. I could feel eyes on me from every angle, people curious to see someone like me for the first time, I assumed!

Geremiah recognized my nervousness, patting me on the shoulder. "It's going to be okay!"

I nodded hesitantly, sitting down at the table Geremiah picked out for us, waiting for the manager to come. I scanned the restaurant, watching the different people working there, each doing a different job—very different from Vietnam where most of the food places were on the streets—street vendors with one person doing everything from cooking to serving to cashiering! There must have been at least over ten people working at this restaurant. The smell of the food served at Wendy's was very strong and flavorful. Meat burning on the grill, soda pop in dispensing machines—everything was so foreign to me but fascinating.

"We might have to wait a little longer, Hoan. It looks like they are very busy," Geremiah told me, as if expecting me to understand all of it. Luckily, he was really efficient and effective with his hand signs by this time, pointing to his watch as I nodded, smiling.

I continued to take in the aroma of the food at Wendy's, my mind drifting back to my home far away!

*****

"That was a great movie, right?" I said excitedly to the group.

"I thought it was a little slow, and the characters were not quite developed deep enough," our expert movie critic, Lan, complained.

"Well, I thought it was pretty good, Hoan," Thao spoke up, always happy to contradict Phuong.

Diep, Nhat, and I speculated they had a "thing" for each other but wouldn't dare tell them. Knowing Lan, she would tear us apart, limb from limb! Instead, we looked at each other, smiling in acknowledgment of the secret between the three of us.

"Let's get something to eat! How about some rice porridge? There's a good one down the street." Diep broke the awkward silence between Lan and Thao, who were now just staring at each other!

We all said in unison, "Sounds good!" as we jumped back on our bikes, heading down the street from the movie theater for a late-night snack.

The vendor, a woman in her sixties, shouted out Diep's name as we got off our bikes. He was a regular!

*****

"Good morning. How are you gentlemen doing?" A tall, big-looking man with a low, strong, robust voice woke me up instantly from my very brief daydream.

"We are fine. How are you?" Geremiah responded, obviously doing all the talking for us since the few words I knew wouldn't contribute anything useful to this conversation.

"How can I help you today?" he asked.

"This is Hoan, and I am Geremiah, a deacon at Saint Francis Catholic Church. Hoan is a refugee from Vietnam, and Father Flannagan at the church wants to see if he's able to have a job here at Wendy's," Geremiah said gently, cracking a big smile at the end.

"Bill, I am the manager here. We can always use some help here! Does he speak any English?"

"No, not really. But he can and is willing to work very hard!" Geremiah again patted me on the shoulder.

"Well, we can have him clean up tables, sweep and mop the floors, and take out the trash in back. I'll be right back with an application, and you can fill it out for him!"

"Are you okay?" Geremiah asked as Bill left to get the application.

I nodded yes, feeling a little nervous still. I haven't worked a day in my life up until now, and all that was about to change. I was really growing up, taking care of myself and making a new life. I held back tears as visions of my mom and siblings, my friends, my home, and my beloved country invaded my thoughts. I scanned around the restaurant one more time, realizing both of us were so different—an Ethiopian and a Vietnamese in a fast-food restaurant in Kansas City. I promised myself right then and there that this would be a great start to a new life. I had no choice but to make it work. It was not about me. It was about family, a new future, human endurance, and the unwavering human spirit, and I was smack in the middle of this new adventure! Life moved on as if nothing happened prior to me coming here. Nobody knew me here, nobody knew the circumstances, and nobody seemed interested in knowing. I looked at Geremiah, still smiling. He was not only part of the sponsoring family; he quickly became a really good, caring friend, my first *real* friend in America.

Bill came back to the table. Geremiah was looking way more anxious than I was. "He got the job! It will be the minimum wage. Since he can't speak much English, as we talked earlier, we will have him clean the tables, the floor, take out the trash—things like that."

"He will do anything you ask him to!" Geremiah answered for me, smiling broadly.

Bill shook my hand. "Welcome to Wendy's, young man!" He waved another young man over. "This is Mike. He will show you everything you need to do. Mike, this is Hoan. He just came to Kansas City and will be a part of our family."

"Hi, I'm Mike. Welcome to Kansas City. Nice to meet you, and welcome to Wendy's. Hope you will like it here. We will go through everything you need to do—clocking in, uniforms, hours, etc. If you have any questions at all, don't hesitate to ask." Mike welcomed me with a firm handshake. He was tall and skinny—well, tall to me anyway.

"Hoan doesn't speak much English. So if you can show him and speak slowly to help him, that would be great. He just came to America and is in the process of learning our language," Geremiah explained to Mike.

"No problem. He's in good hands, and I will help him in any way I can." Mike smiled genuinely. That day, I made another good friend, Mike. A new life was starting to take shape.

"Thanks Geremiah. Since you said he has English classes Mondays, Wednesdays, and Fridays, he can work with us Tuesdays, Thursdays, and Saturdays. Does that work?" Bill said, handing Geremiah a form. "If that's okay, you can fill out this form for him, and we will see him next Tuesday."

"That's great. Thank you, Bill. It will only take a minute for me to fill out this form and give it to you here. Hoan will be here next Tuesday!" Geremiah said, excitedly shaking Bill's hand.

"Thank you, Bill and Mike!" I managed to say the only few words I knew, smiling.

We headed out of Wendy's into the white stuff again, Geremiah's right arm crossing my shoulders.

"Thank you, Geremiah, for helping me!" I said, wondering what it would be like working at Wendy's, not knowing the language well. I decided to deal with that problem when I got to it. It might be a good opportunity for me to practice what I learned in Sister Claire's English class.

I smiled, walking with Geremiah to the car, flakes of more white stuff falling densely on top of our heads. For the first time, I did not feel cold. I did not feel out of place. I did not feel like an outsider. It was a *new beginning*! This is the day I started building a new life in a new homeland. When I look back upon this day years later, it will always be one of my fondest memories. The struggles diminished, however slightly, giving way to something happier, more peaceful. But the memories of home, relatives and friends, teachers, and neighbors would always weigh heavy on me for the rest of my life. What would become of everyone I grew up loving and depending on? I was afraid, as with anything, that time would eventually erase the endearing images of a time that was. I felt a sense of profound sadness as I stepped into the big yellow car. I was afraid that what I heard from Mom and Dad long ago would come true: "*Life goes on!*"

And went on, it did. For the next several months, I would make the thirty-minute walk every Tuesday, Thursday, and Saturday from the project to Wendy's downtown to work in my fake white boots. They did look stylish for a young boy but were a piece of shit when it came to keeping my feet warm! I remember coming to work at least thirty minutes early to allow my toes to regain their consciousness before getting to work. The work was very hard—rolling trash cans much bigger and heavier than me outside in the cold white stuff and dumping them in huge containers. But it was the kind of hard work that marked the start of a new life of a boy coming into adulthood.

It would get easier! I told myself.

It never did, but I was happy to take it on.

CHAPTER 22

Passage of Time

Years had passed since time slowly eased the emotional pain of change, of goodbyes. People I knew moved on with their lives, losing touch with one another as the demands of life required their full attention. The older parents passed away; the young children probably married and had children of their own. Through it all, there had been one constant: *change!* Time was and is at the center of all things—memories faded, emotional scars healed, and new life experiences took shape. I often wondered about the what-ifs.

What would life have been without the devastating war, tearing families apart, pushing people away from the life they had always known, casting them to places far away, knowing nothing and no one? What would my life have become if I was still there in my homeland, making new friends and growing old with old friends?

It had been a long time since my first day on my very first job in America at Wendy's. I had lived new experiences, met new people, lived a new way of life, and spoken a new language since the day that scared, uninspired little boy stepped foot in America. The passage of time pushed me, nurtured me, challenged me, and inspired me to start a new life. While there are no regrets, I will carry the what-ifs for a long time to come. But I knew deep down that I had to face what is and not worry about the what-if. I had lived a *blessed life*, becoming a successful, contributing member of society, teaching college at age twenty-five, and helping others adapt and assimilate into society as I did years ago. There are many more stories to tell, many memories to revisit, and many experiences to share.

"Welcome to freedom, young man. *Welcome to your new life*, young man. *Welcome to adulthood*, young man. *Welcome to your future*, young man. *Move forward* and *be happy!"*

Those were the final thoughts I had before putting the past behind me—no more daydreams, no more flashbacks.

Thank you, *America*. Thank you, Mom and Dad. Thank you for getting me on the path to a new life, a *blessed life*!

9 798890 610942